Walk A Narrow Line.
(Because You Can.)

Rod Graham

III Clink
Street

London | New York

Published by Clink Street Publishing 2020

Copyright © 2020

First edition.

ISBN:
978-1-913340-76-6 paperback
978-1-913340-77-3 ebook

Please use this link to download the title track of the album:
Walk A Narrow Line.
http://www.walkanarrowline.com

Please use this link to access the whole album:
Walk A Narrow Line.
http://www.rod-graham.com

Chapter 1

Not for the first time, I was looking at boats; cruisers, to be specific. The more I looked, the stronger became the desire to have another go at boating; to be spending hours lost in the pleasure of a more relaxed world, which is a bit like caravanning, but on water. No one gets tired of that sense of earthiness; the feeling of placidness that being near to rivers and canals can bring; do they? The site and sound of water seem to lend so much healing to your soul.

When I think back to times gone by; if we count our lives like a cat's, after all; I am a Leo; the first boat I ever had was probably in my umpteenth life, with my first wife, Frances, in 1976. It was just a one summer thing. The boat came and went, like the summer; in the blink of an eye. We were a young family with two children, Paula and Trevor.

I don't want to give you the impression that we were well off; just because we bought a boat, far from it, like most people we spent our time ducking and diving… doing a little bit of this or a bit of that, trying to get ahead, looking for a goldmine that would help us earn enough money to pay our way; then guess what; having to pick ourselves up and start all over again.

How often, I wonder, did we manage to deposit any money into the bank account? I always felt such a fraud queuing up in the bank; standing there in my jeans and tee shirt to pay a bill or two; everyone else seemed to look so much more affluent than me. Originally, I'd only opened a bank account to pay in my student grant while at art College in East Ham. Now, I was living in Friern Barnet, trying to make a go of a music shop which we had called *Manuscript*. Not many years before that, I'd had a 'Post Office

Savings Account'; banks were for the rich. Does anyone have a Post Office Savings Account? Back then, you paid whatever money you wanted to save; in to your account each week, if you could afford to. You would go to the Post Office counter, give the cashier your money and they would write into a little savings book, how much money you had paid in; then they would put an official rubber stamp next to the entry. You would keep the savings book in your possession; this book was the only record of how much money you had saved. A bit like a bank but not nearly as sophisticated and certainly with none of the security we need in our modern world; no requests for proof of I.D, proof of age; none of that stuff, just your savings book and a smile.

#

Let me tell you about our first cabin cruiser.

In 1976 we heard about a chap who was selling up to emigrate to Canada, he needed the cash as he was running out of time before his departure, so he would take a mere £50 for his 24ft boat, that we were told had four berths and all mod-cons. Yes, I know what you are thinking…

"Couldn't have been much of a craft for £50."

Right, let's see!

Off we trotted to the river Lea near Broxbourne, in Hertfordshire to see this boat. Now let us remember that we knew nothing about boats or boating, that whole world was a dream to us; we had only ever watched other people living that dream, but it just seemed like a good idea at the time. The music shop we owned (well, we ran the business; the premises were rented) was open all day, Monday to Saturday. Most of my evenings were spent teaching music in the studio at the rear of the shop, Saturday evenings; I would usually go out to play a gig either by myself or with Len's band. Yes, I'm a musician, not only do I teach music, but I play piano, sing and have a pretty cool guitar style.

#

After finishing art college in 1970, I had become a graphic artist for a few years, but when I was replaced by yet another art studio while in Australia, I decided my face just didn't fit in that world. Later, while experimenting with various wheeler dealer schemes there in Australia, which included selling second hand cars, trying to sell my paintings, a second hand furniture shop, subcontract decorating (More about these later!) and doing a milk round (which had to be done at night) in Perth; I fell into playing the guitar and singing with a couple of very nice Aussies who had a function band. It's a funny thing, one of them was from an Italian family; he played and taught the organ. His English wasn't the best and his organ playing could have done with some improvement; I, on the other hand, was lucky enough to have had piano lessons in my younger days and taken all my grades; it had never occurred to me to pass on my music knowledge till I met him. When we came back to England in 1974, I started teaching music. To teach is definitely to learn, it's a wonderful life.

#

That 1976 summer was proving to be a really hot one; it's on record as being one of the driest summers we've had; which is interesting because we had never heard of 'climate change' in 1976, it was just a great summer. If you thought about it; you could just imagine yourself jumping in to the river off a boat deck, splashing about in the water, creating waves, wild swimming, the whole scene seemed to beckon ever harder with each longing thought you gave it.

This cabin cruiser was no *Queen Mary*, what did you expect for £50 in 1976? She was made of wood; marine ply, to be exact, you could be forgiven for being apprehensive about stepping aboard her, after all, wood was the customary material used to build boats for years. However, this particular craft may have been one of Noah's castoffs; except that he probably didn't have access to what looked like white emulsion paint. The whole boat had been liberally coated in it, you could see that someone had done a real quick job of freshening her up with a very clumsy hand and brush; even the windows had not been spared a daub or two of paint.

Our son Trevor; who was eleven years old at the time, couldn't contain his excitement at the thought of this adventure. On to the boat he jumped right behind Nigel, the owner, a scruffy guy with long greasy brown hair, who was either a really good salesman or very proud of his vessel. He certainly had the gift of the gab. My wife Frances and I gave each other a sidelong look of disappointment at the sight of this shipwreck. My heart sank; like this boat probably would. I remember thinking, 'what a mess; well... one man's meat is another man's poison'. Still; we both tried to keep an open mind.

There were indeed four bunks, which, amazingly, all seemed to be dry, there was a galley area with a gas cooker and sink. Nigel told us that you call the kitchen area 'The Galley' on a boat. There was a cassette toilet that smelt and looked a bit like an old-fashioned sewerage farm with a small sink for washing beside it. The mirror above the sink was interesting in that you couldn't actually see your reflection in it properly for grime. I turned around and looked to make sure Nigel wasn't watching me as I quickly drew a smiley face on the mirror's dirty surface. I'm lucky in that I have a fairly good memory for faces; especially mine! The thing is, if you wanted to clean yourself up, comb your hair, shave or make yourself look pretty; you were going to need a good memory for faces with this mirror. The shipwreck did have a nice sitting area at the back, or stern if I'm to be correct with an outboard motor that had its own removable fuel tank, I noticed that Nigel didn't offer to start the engine; he just pointed it out, saying that it was a good runner. But no matter, as this trip looked like it had been a waste of time anyway.

We climbed off the boat, although I had to practically drag Trevor off, as he already thought he owned it and was involved with cruising down the Caribbean, so he had a reluctance to end his adventure; Paula had not dared to come aboard, she remained on dry land pretending to be disinterested as she stroked someone's golden Labrador that had wandered over inquiringly from another boat.

I told Nigel that we would like to look around, as there were other boats for sale in the marina.

Well, after looking over a few of those boats and hearing the amazing sums of money their owners were hoping to sell them for; it has to be said that *Willie* – that is what the shipwreck was called – started to look like a good proposition; after all, beggars can't be choosers, she was still afloat, she had an engine and was dry-ish inside; we could hopefully make something of her.

Back to see Nigel we went, then after a bit of haggling for the boat and for the mooring which was rented, we were shortly the proud owners of *Willie* our very own cabin cruiser.

Every Sunday for the rest of that long hot summer would find us doing what must have been the equivalent of an hours training in a gym; just pulling the cord trying to start that outboard motor. Messing about on the river usually had to wait a while! Some days though, things would be messier than others.

There was that time when our daughter, Paula; who was a year older than Trevor; got a little too boisterous in the stern section and nearly fell overboard. Yes, she could swim but we were cruising along with the outboard motor running at the time and she went over the stern right beside it. As I watched her loose her balance, I had visions of my daughter being chewed up by the engine propeller. Don't ask me how, but I turned around from steering the boat and caught her in mid-air before she even hit the water and hauled her back into the boat. It was one of those moments of magic. I have no idea what happened, or how I managed it, just like when you knock something off a shelf by accident, then react so fast, that with no effort at all, you actually catch it before it hits the floor and breaks, I expect you will have done that yourself.

Can you believe that one Sunday evening when it was getting late before we packed our things and set off home, we actually forgot to put Monty, our border collie into the car? It wasn't until I had driven the fourteen miles home that we realised he was missing. Now Monty was a bit of a guard dog and not very good with strangers, (as you will learn later in the book) so our car may have exceeded the speed limit a little bit on the way back to the marina to get him; we certainly couldn't get back there quick enough for fear of him doing someone some damage. Fortunately, it was a very quiet Sunday evening on the roads so we got to the marina in record time and there was Monty, sitting in the stern of the boat like a Captain, as if nothing had happened, completely oblivious to our forgetfulness.

The River Lea was always so placid, none of the world's hubbub; just a beautiful summer, with a sun that seemed endless, in a mythical time. When, in the evening, that sun did start to go down, you would have to squint at the light as it bounced across the surface of the water. We would sit in silence with a glass of something pleasantly refreshing to drink, listening to the gentle murmur of a soft breeze as it swished through the vegetation, watching the reflections of the reeds on the opposite bank as they danced on the glass like surface of the water. There were a couple of swans who would often visit the boats accompanied by two signets who were quite big, but still had their brown under feathers, looking to see if anyone had any scraps of food; have you ever noticed how angry the queen's birds can look close up.

Well, those memories of a long-lost summer, though nearly forty years ago or however long ago, can pull at your heartstrings, stretch you're longing like a sock and fill your dreams with anticipation. What are we if we cannot dream and scheme, if we cannot think of another mountain worth the climbing, then set off in search of our goal?

Chapter 2

So, here we were in a new century, 2003 to be precise, looking up at an eight-meter Seamaster cruiser. We were in York, which is on the River Ouse. It was the end of March and despite the weather throwing us some cold winds and rain, I thought that buying a boat at this time of year would give us a good spring, plus a full summer for cruising and messing about.

The men from the boatyard had craned the six-ton cruiser out of the water and propped it up on the hard standing with blocks and timbers, to enable the surveyor to look over the hull properly. The hull also needed a fresh coat of 'antifoul paint' to inhibit the growth of weed and algae.

She was made of fibreglass, which is what they call 'plastic', that is to say she was not a wood or steel boat. When you first see a boat like this out of the water, it looks huge, almost like a small liner; well this being a new experience, it did to us. Amazing to think that if our surveyor gave her a good report, we were actually going to buy this craft. She was just over eight metres long and about thirty years old; her name was *Harnser.*

#

I thought back to 1957 and the workman's punt on the River Colne in Denham. That was the first boat I had ever messed about with. I must apologies now; finally; because when the workmen went home at the end of the day and at the weekends; they used to hide their punt among the reeds they were clearing, but Kenny Wolacott, who was a childhood friend of mine and I, used to look for it and find it. We had great fun with that little boat, and then one day we actually sunk it. We never did find out if the workmen retrieved it from the river bed.

Chapter 3

This is probably a good time to tell you a bit about the children's home I was in for two years at Denham in Buckinghamshire.

Usually, there were about forty of us kids in the home. When I first got sent there in 1956 at age thirteen, there were half a dozen girls living there as well as the boys. If you think about it, you'll see that the lads outnumbered the lasses about eight to one, which proved to be a recipe for disaster. No; I don't mean a disaster for the boys. Some of us more adventurous lads enjoyed ourselves showing off to these females, or we sneaked over to their dormitory after lights out. Unfortunately, there were also some arguments and fights, especially over who's girlfriend Diane actually was.

Did I hear you ask "What about the other girls?"

Well; Diane was probably the oldest and although most of the more mature lads fancied her, it was rumoured that she was Ginger's older brother Kenny's girlfriend and most of the lads were scared of him as he had a bad reputation. Only thing was; that Kenny had been in hospital for quite a while and was away convalescing after some weird illness. At that time, I'd never met him anyway, so; nothing to be scared of. Besides; when the cats away... I won't go into that, but sad to say, it was not very long before the girls were sent elsewhere to live and it became a boy's only home.

It was called Denham Court. We were all under the care of the Middlesex County Council. I had been placed in to the care and protection of the council nearly four years earlier, when I was nine years old. This home was managed by Mr Hill, who; was a tall man, but probably because he ran the place with a rod of iron; seemed to us lads to be about seven foot tall. The boys were terrified of him. He had grey hair, glasses, and a voice like a cannon. We called him 'Man Hill'. Not to his face of course, you would have got a thump and put on a punishment for that if he heard you. His wife, who we hardly ever saw; was supposed to be the matron, they had a daughter called Peggy, who was always standoffish and never spoke to us lads, I think she went to a private school and thought herself above us.

That was one of the things about Denham Court; we all went off each day to different schools. Not like the boarding school which I had been sent to three years before going to Denham Court. I was the only boy from the children's home who went to Alderbourne County which was a brand-new school built just outside Denham Village in 1956.

When Kenny Wolacott eventually came out of convalescence, he was sent to the same school as me for a while, but he got poorly with kidney trouble and was taken off to hospital. I didn't see him again for quite a long time, which was a pity, as he had overlooked my trying it on with his girlfriend, Diane; and we had become very close friends. You don't make really good friends every day, do you? Before Kenny turned up, his younger brother Ginger and I used to knock about together, but Kenny was the one I really clicked with, because we both had the devil and the same sense of mischief in us. As you will see, he popped in and out of my life for a number of years.

The only other members of staff were 'Old Man Chappell' and of course, the cook, who was a little grey-haired Chinese lady with a terrible temper. We all had to take our turn at being in the kitchen to help out by doing the washing up and we were always careful not to upset her. If you did, she would rage on and on at you in her native tongue, you couldn't understand a word. She caught me once with a pocketful of raisins that I had robbed from a barrel in the pantry and Kenny had a couple of eggs that we were going to throw at the local gamekeeper's dog if it barked at us when we were in the woods. This little Chinese lady, who was really slight, being only about four foot tall, would place herself uncomfortably close to you, wagging her forefinger in your face as she told you off; your ears would ring with the shrillness of her voice. I still can't speak Chinese.

There are things to tell about 'Old Man Chappell'; I will tell you more later.

The house at Denham, (maybe I should call it a mansion) looked like it had once been a stately home. The huge downstairs rooms, one of which housed two full-sized billiard tables and a table tennis table, all had oak panelled walls. We were all convinced that behind one of the panels was a secret passage where Charles's cavaliers had hidden from the roundheads. There was a room at the side of the home which had windows all round, looking out over the extensive lawns to the River Colne.

Nearby to Denham was an American airbase, whose personnel would come to the home a few times each year to throw a party for us lads. They would use this room as a dance hall. The airmen would bring a record player with them and all the latest American rock and roll records. (Rock and roll was in its infancy and was only just starting to get airplay on the radio on this country's one popular music channel which was called *BBC The Light Programme.*)

The house had a wide staircase leading upstairs from the grand entrance hallway. I never saw the front doors used as we only ever used the back door. Prior to becoming a children's home, it had been used as a reform school for a while. That was an institution where naughty kids were sent for correction. If you have a look now, you will see that it has become 'The Buckinghamshire Golf Club'. You can book wedding receptions, functions and conferences there; it is very grand. This is not supposed to be an advert for the place, but do go on; take a look and you will see what a splendid house and gardens we lived in. Of course, being children; I'm not sure that we appreciated it on that level. Most of us lads couldn't wait to get away from the place when we left school.

The school leaving age was fifteen in 1958 when I left school; it was raised to sixteen in 1972, then raised again in 2013 to age seventeen and finally in 2015 it was raised to eighteen years of age. I'll never forget the day I left Denham Court at age fifteen to catch a train bound for London then subsequently East Finchley and the Wards, who would be my first foster parents. Rather than give me and my suitcases; one of which was nearly as big as me; a ride, the two miles of country road to Harefield station in his Ford Prefect car; on this scorching hot August day; Old Man Hill made me walk. I can remember looking back at him as I trundled up the treelined drive (which was a mile long), with my suitcases and seeing him standing at the bottom of the drive with his hands on his hips watching me struggle. It amused me a bit because each time I looked back at him, he got smaller and smaller as the distance between us increased. I swear he didn't like me; he always appeared to have a sneer on his face when he talked to me. I think it had something to do with me having piano lessons and needing to practice for my exams, as I was the only boy given permission to go into the sun parlour, which was used as a music room to play a piano that had been especially procured for me. I always felt that he resented me for that.

It really was a beautiful day though, made better by the thought of leaving Denham Court. Luckily; trains used to be fairly frequent at country stations, so it didn't matter to me how long I took to get there. I rested quite a few times to get my strength back as those cases were both really heavy. The larger of the two had my clothes in. The smaller one held my massive collection of Meccano, parts of which Old Man Chappell had bought me, it was the original metal kind that some of you might remember. I've never forgiven 'Man Hill' for that piece of unkindness. Then again; it was probably one of those character-building episodes you get in life.

Chapter 4

That'll do for now; let me tell you some more about *Harnser*, the boat we bought in Naburn near York in 2003.

Well; the boat surveyor gave *Harnser* a clean bill of health so we purchased her. I am only going to tell you one story about this craft, for although it was a nice boat; we didn't keep her for more than a few months. It seems that with boats; as with anything; buying second, third or even fourth hand, can mean you might have a lot of improvement work to do. Hopefully; someone else is enjoying her now.

The men at the boatyard craned *Harnser* back into the river for us after I'd antifouled the hull. It was late march 2003, there had been some rain but the weather on this day looked pretty good.

My first wife and I had an amicable divorce in 1981. My second wife, Ruth and I got together in 1983. The reason I have told you that now is because Ruth and I have two daughters, Danielle and Stephanie. In 2003 when we bought *Harnser* Danni, the oldest, was eleven years old. The same age as my son Trevor had been when I bought my first boat down in Hertfordshire in 1976.

Harnser now had to be cruised from York to Ripon where we had rented a mooring, a distance of approximately fifty kilometres. What a fabulous feeling that was. Stepping aboard our own craft and heading off to do a real cruise by boat; not like the messing about we used to do with *Willie* on the same half mile or so of the river Lea. Oh yes, the River Lea 1976; a beautiful placid piece of water, nothing like the river experience my daughter and I were about so face on the flooded River Ouse and the River Ure in Yorkshire.

I definitely felt like a Captain with a crew of one; who was our lovely, eleven-year-old daughter Danielle. We filled the tank up with red diesel, made sure that there was Calor gas and water, stowed away the provisions and bedding we had bought with us, untied the mooring ropes and away we went. The trip was going to take just under two days.

The River Ouse was peaceful and wide, as we left Naburn, heading for the centre of York. I felt a tinge of disappointment that we weren't doing this on a glorious summer's day. The only other boats we saw were moored up or resting on the banks, still in hibernation from the winter. We were looking at a grey, very early spring afternoon. It felt surreal, almost ominous, being the only boat on such a large deserted river, I found myself wondering if the other boaters knew something that we didn't. Maybe a river monster had been seen and reported in the local paper. Should we have bought the local rag and scanned it for river news just in case? No of course not; we were probably just the first boaters to brave a trip by water this year.

As I was unsure of the way to Ripon by river; I had confirmed with Gary, the boat salesman in the yard that we just needed to follow the river upstream. My research had told me that there were four locks to negotiate before we reached Ripon. I could see that we were cruising against the current and marvelled at the way *Harnser* was handling the flow. It would take us about an hour before we were cruising through the centre of York.

Through the City of York we went, under the bridges, seeing the traffic above, noticing the people walking about, feeling very proud of ourselves, Rulers of the river. Look at the peasants on foot and in cars! Danni and I owned the river. Even the moorings at Museum Gardens that are so often packed with narrow boats and cruisers during the summer months were deserted. 'Ha ha this is grand.' We had been to York many times and watched the boating folk nonchalantly cruising up and down, looking like a different race of people than us and feeling a twang of jealousy as we silently wished that we could be one of them, well, now we were.

There had been some rain lately, as you would expect from late winter. It started to drizzle again now; Danni helped me to pull the canopy up so that we wouldn't get wet. That caused our first problem, because the windscreen and side windows immediately started to steam up, there being no demisters on a boat like this. The wipers were inefficiently slow at sweeping across the windscreen, we were lucky to get about one wipe per minute. When it became too difficult to see where we were going, we developed a system whereby the crew member cleared the windscreen using a towel. It was a good job there were no other boats on the river, as we were all over the place for a while and boats; unlike cars, are supposed to drive on the right or starboard side of the waterway to avoid collisions with craft coming the other way. I have since learnt to avoid cruising in the rain, it being mostly a fair-weather activity. Still we carried on, as we were now committed to getting *Harnser* to Ripon and our new mooring.

Our next problem came when we reached Nun Monkton about an hour after passing through York. I should have studied my geography more closely or at least had a map. There is a fork in the river at Nun Monkton, I knew that; the River Ouse takes a sharp right-hand turn. If you keep going straight you will go up the river Nidd, which runs down to the Ouse at this point and is not normally navigable by a boat of our size, not by any boat normally. Today, however; was an exception. I did not realise that the water level had risen and the river was so much higher than normal. I had no concept in my head that the river was still rising, owing to the rain that had fallen over the last few days. Yes, it is a fact that we should have been aware of. When there is rain, it makes its way down from the high ground, on its journey to the sea and the river can fill up quite quickly. I thought the water would take days to get down to the river. What a pity Gary, the boat salesman, had not warned us. What a pity I was so eager to get cruising that I had not done my homework thoroughly enough.

As we approached a junction in the river; I looked to the right and with some difficulty, through the misted windows, I could see a waterway going between the trees in that direction, but there seemed to be too much vegetation growing across the river to make it navigable. The channel that went straight ahead looked like the best option for a boat, so I came to the conclusion that this could not be the place where the Ouse bends off to the right, we must not have got that far yet. I steered *Harnser* straight ahead, up what I now know is the river Nidd. I remember thinking to myself, "Gosh, the river has got narrow all of a sudden and what a lot of vegetation and weed in the water."

Well; it was not long before the river reduced in size to a very large stream and then to a small stream. The depth gauge on *Harnser* started to beep a shallow water warning. At least it's working, I thought.

It was obvious now; that we had gone the wrong way. The only snag was how to go back the way we had come. The River Nidd was far too narrow to allow us to turn the boat around. There was only one thing to do. Reverse! That was easier said than done, as we had cruised quite a way up the flooded Nidd, not helped by the poor visibility through our windscreen. I found that the boat actually steered quite well in reverse, lucky for us. The main thing I was concerned about was running aground or getting the propeller chocked with weed.

After a few mishaps we managed to get ourselves back on to the River Ouse. Then we found ourselves laughing at the silly navigation mistake I'd made and perhaps smiling with relief at still being afloat. Our adventure was still on course.

It was about five-thirty in the evening; we were starting to lose the light. Surely the first lock at Linton can't be far now. Linton Lock with its lock house and pub was going to be our overnight stop.

There are a lot of trees on either side of the river along this stretch. Many of the trees had their feet standing in the flood water. Beningbrough Hall, which is a National Trust property, is off to the right. There are red and green navigation buoys to warn of sand banks and shallow water. I knew to keep the red buoys to my right (starboard), the green buoys to my left (port) going up stream. Thing was, that with the light fading fast, they were not easy to see.

Finally, we came around a bend, out of the trees and there it was at last, with welcoming lights shimmering in the distance; Linton Lock. Now; do not be tempted to head straight for the lock by cutting across the wide bend in the river as you approach Linton. It may look tempting, but follow the marker buoys, keep to your starboard side as this is where the deep water is. Someone once tried cutting across in a narrow boat, ran aground and had to spend a week stuck on the sand bank, waiting for it to rain so the water depth would rise enough to float them off. The lock keeper was kindly ferrying supplies over to them in his rowing boat. That must have been interesting; living in the middle of the river all week with everyone who passed knowing that you had tried to take a short cut to the lock.

By the time we reached the lock at Linton, the lock keeper was not happy to let us go into the lock as the daylight had gone and it could be dangerous. He advised us to moor up below the lock on the floating pontoon. A pontoon of this type is designed to float up and down with the rise and fall of the river, helping to keep your craft afloat with the different water levels.

Danni and I had a nice evening meal of chicken and chips in the pub at the lock side and then retired to *Harnser.* As we bedded down you could see the white foam from the weir, which was beside the lock; this is where the river flows around the actual lock cut. The water was flowing over the top of the weir, then crashing down about three feet, making so much noise that we found it hard to sleep. Still we felt secure with the boat tied up safely to the floating pontoon.

The next day presented us with a beautiful, bright early spring morning, a bit cold, but never mind. The first thing that struck me on waking up was the silence. Something was missing. Then, when I opened the curtains on *Harnser* we saw the reason. There was no longer a weir. The river had risen so much overnight, that instead of falling three feet, the water was just pouring over the remaining lip of the weir construction. To see the width of the river now and the force of the water rushing down it was frightening. The pontoon had risen up with the water and was much higher than the night before but at least our boat seemed to be secure. So, Danni and I got ourselves up, dressed and had breakfast before going to see the lock keeper.

The lock keeper was an amicable chap called Ian. We had a chat and a laugh the evening before so were on good terms. He came out of his lock house, took one look at the river's height and shook his head in dismay. The thought of getting the boat into the lock against that current was worrying us both. However, I kept my apprehension to myself as I didn't want to alarm Danni. I was determined; we were going to arrive at Ripon Racecourse Marina today, if Noah could do it; so could we; besides, I had work commitments that needed my attention at home. I managed to convince Ian that if he helped us, we could easily manage to get our boat in to the lock. So, Danni and I hurried down to *Harnser*, while Ian opened the lower lock gates for us. I started the engine and off we went towards the lock entrance.

The current was indeed very fierce. *Harnser*'s diesel engine had to push with all its might to make headway against the water. I got Danni to throw a rope from the bow of the boat up to Ian who was leaning over the lock side, to help pull us through the gates into the lock. Because the river had swollen so much, it was not far for her to throw. It took a few attempts but finally we made it into the safety of Linton Lock. We tied *Harnser* up to the mooring pontoon and breathed a sigh of relief, wishing we had come into the lock the night before. I suppose 'If only's' don't count for much in life. I looked over the lock gates at the roaring torrent below that we had just escaped from. Well, at least we were safe.

From the lock side, looking down the lock cut, you would never guess the state of the river running around it, everything looked so calm. Some years before; this whole area had been flooded, including the lock house. There is a plaque on the wall to show how high the water has risen on various occasions. British Waterways have carried out a lot of work over the years to try and tame the river; with some success.

Chapter 5

I was just thinking about how we learn from others; not only the good things but, the bad things as well. History has shown us that. Unfortunately, I don't think I learnt very much from my mum and dad. Apparently; she left him and went back to her home in Cornwall when I was about two years old, taking me with her after placing my three-year-old sister in a London convent. Ok; we had been war babies, they'd probably had one of those rushed war time marriages you hear about, where people met and were worried that they may not have any tomorrow; so, they lived for the day. I don't really know, I'm just guessing; they seemed so mismatched and neither of them would discuss the past with me. In 1945, it might well have been the right thing for her to do; getting away from London for a while.

My mum was called Ruby, she was a singer, she would sing with dance bands that were fashionable at the time. Unfortunately, most of her work was in London, so that is where she chose to return after leaving me as a two-year-old, to be looked after by her brother and his wife in Cornwall.

Ruby's brother and his wife did, apparently, look after me for a while, but then passed me on to someone else, who eventually passed me on to someone else. Apparently, I spent the next three years being passed around to different people down in Cornwall. Of course, I only have vague memories of being that young; this is mostly stuff that people have told me in later years. Although, I have to say; that you do remember the odd little thing from when you were small, don't you? I remember a place that had outside stairs going up to the front door. I remember a collie dog that I loved to cuddle and stroke, probably the only affection that I could find, his name was Collin and I would often get told off for feeding him under the table at meal times. Memories of that lovely dog always made me want one of my own. I remember a family who had two children whose toys I wasn't allowed to play with; if I did take an interest in a toy, one of these kids would squawk to their mother and I would be told to leave it alone. Maybe I was a destructive kid, I have no idea! I don't even remember who they were. Perhaps I made it up! Strange things to have a memory of!

Well, I certainly don't remember Ruby, my mother, not from those early years. She remained an enigma to me for the rest of her life. I didn't meet her again until I was thirty-eight years old and that was more or less by chance; but still, even as an adult, I was unable to understand the person who bore me in to the world, she was a closed book and would always elude me, as you will see later.

Chapter 6

This March morning in 2003, Danni and I sat in the lock cut at Linton, having a cup tea and a biscuit. The sky was blue, the sun was shining, it seemed a shame not to take advantage of the good weather and the river didn't look too swollen from here. I started *Harnser*'s engine, Danni untied the ropes and hopped aboard; off we went.

It wasn't until we got to the entrance of the lock cut and steered into the river that we saw the extent of the flood. The river wasn't flowing so fast that we couldn't make headway against the current, there was just a lot of water and it looked very much like we had suddenly arrived on to a massive lake. You could only see where the river should have been, by the tops of trees that would normally line the banks and were now sticking up out of the water. Either side of the trees the flood extended quite some way into the fields. Oh well! We were in a boat, so heart in mouth, let's push on. I hate to imagine what would have happened if the engine had failed, the only other sign of life being Ian; the lock keeper and he was back there somewhere snug in the lock house.

It took us about an hour and three quarters, pushing the current, to arrive at Milby Lock, in Boroughbridge, which is the next lock you come to when heading up river. There were no moorings to be seen anywhere, it was obvious that they were under water. So, I steered *Harnser* over to the very steep grass bank just outside the lock gates, jumped off onto the grass, hammered a couple of mooring spikes into the ground to tie the boat up to, then it was lunch time.

We have cycled from Ripon to Boroughbridge and seen this

lock from the road, so I knew the river must have risen by at least a metre and a half. Realising that was enough, but glancing back down the river we had just cruised up, all you could see were white water rapids. That is how fast it was flowing on the narrow approach to the lock. There is only a short lock cut at the bottom of Milby Lock, but we were safe enough here, out of the current. We felt like explorers having beans on toast, a mug of tea and watching a few people walking their dogs. Marvellous!

Under normal river conditions I think Milby Lock is probably about two metres deep when empty. Danni and I only had to lower the water level about half a metre, before we could open the lower lock gate to enter it. That tells you how high the river was.

We left Milby Lock heading on up river for the town of Boroughbridge. With the river level being so high, air clearance on the road bridge at Boroughbridge looked very low as we approached it. In fact, as we got nearer, Danni looked at me in a panic and shouted, "We'll never fit under it, dad!"

Well; sometimes I'm a gung-ho type of guy and we were pushing a heavy current, I couldn't stop the boat or we would have been taken back by the flow. So, I tried to gauge the highest part of the bridge and went for it. Oops, there was a loud bang as the bridge knocked our radio aerial off the roof. Luckily, we had lowered the canopy, as it was a nice day; otherwise the bridge would have ripped it off. Phew! Deep breath, we were out the other side. Hairy moment there for a while and very strange looking at the underside of a bridge so close, you could have admired the engineering work or even painted it, had you the time.

Harnser took us on up river heading for the third lock at Westwick. The River Ouse had become the River Ure now with the water level not appearing to be as high along this stretch, maybe because the banks are higher. Boroughbridge Marina is off to port. There are some tidy houses on the starboard side, looking in danger of being flooded, then a really high road bridge taking the A1 motorway over our heads. We could hear the noise of the traffic even above the roar of our own engine.

All the while the river twists and turns, it's quite magnificent.

We saw a kingfisher shoot past us, scooping the surface of the water, looking for fish, just a flash of blue and then it was gone. A water vole or maybe a rat, looking homeless on the flooded river bank, where their nests must have been, but there was no sign of human life. The water level definitely appeared to be lower now, but I think it was just an illusion, because when we reached Westwick Lock, an hour or so later, once again there were no moorings to be seen; everything was submerged under water.

Harnser had to be moored up somewhere so that we could operate the lock. A huge torrent of water was hitting us on our starboard side from the river that was feeding around the lock cut. I should have steered against it and headed for the quiet pool in front of the lock gates. You would not admire my boat steering skills. The current took me by surprise and pushed *Harnser* right over to port and nearly into the field which was under water. Luckily for us, a barbed wire fence held as we were pushed into it and stopped the boat. Well, that and the fact that we had run aground on what we now know are the concrete moorings which were hiding under the water. There we were stuck.

As we had never been to Westwick Lock before, we had no knowledge of the moorings we had run aground on below the lock. Later that year, however, when out cruising, we discovered that the moorings were concrete and for many months you could still see a long blue skid mark across the top of them which was the evidence of us running aground there. The blue was from the antifoul paint which had been scraped off the hull of *Harnser* by the concrete.

Can you imagine it, 3 pm in the afternoon, it was the middle of March, the day wasn't as bright as it had been; there is a house about 200 metres away on the hill, but no sign of life, I suspected that It might be a holiday cottage. Danielle, who was eleven, and I, half way into a field, on a large boat, looking lost, wondering how we are going to re-float it. In my head desperation was taking over.

"Don't panic, stay calm, let young Danni think you know what you are doing; this is just part of the fun."

I didn't fancy getting into the water, it looked about chest deep and I knew very well that it would be freezing cold. We needed something long to try and push ourselves off against the barbed wire fence in order to re-float *Harnser* again, but what? Even if I'd had tools with me, what sort of tool would that be? Danni found what was needed in the form of an old mop that was hiding in the cabin cupboard. I didn't want her to be the one leaning over the bow, pushing on the fence with a mop that would be too dangerous for her, so I showed her how to operate the control to reverse the boat engine.

The plan being, that Danni would power the boat in reverse, while I pushed against the fence with the mop. Ok, so; while Danni tried reversing *Harnser*, I used the mop to push against the fence where it was within reach and of course, with our weight, being about five tons, the whole fence just seemed to stretch and lean over away from us. For a minute, it looked as though the fence would give way. I shouted back to Danni, "Pull the lever right back."

She revved the engine a bit more but not enough,

"Harder," I shouted, getting a little annoyed.

I could see her yank the throttle lever right back; the boat jumped into life and re-floated with a huge jolt which almost threw me overboard and a scrapping sound from underneath. I had forgotten to tell Danni to shut the throttle off as soon as we got free and we were now shooting backwards against the current, across the river at some speed. Even more annoyed; I hurried round the deck to the stern, shouting for her to push the lever back to the middle, which is neutral, but she couldn't hear me very well above the engine noise. I reached the controls just as she understood me and pushed the throttle in to neutral, so, quickly taking over, I steered us into the calm pool right in front of the lock gates where I should have steered for in the first place. We moored against the island which is formed by the river and the lock cut.

Poor Danni; I looked round from tying a mooring rope to a tree, she was in tears. I climbed back aboard and tried to comfort her.

"We are safe now," I said. "You did really well," giving her a daddy love and cuddle.

I can't tell you how awful I felt. Introducing my young daughter to this river was like a baptism of fire for us both. The stress of it all was just too much and she had broken down in tears of relief. Once again, we had to laugh at ourselves, what on earth were we doing out here on the river, in this weather, just the two of us, no experience of boating on a flooded river. It was actually pretty cool; not that I would want to do it quite like that again.

I think that being a parent is not just about being older and maybe wiser than your child; hopefully you will help them build their confidence in themselves and lead by example. I'm afraid that our little trip up the river may have left my daughter with a bad taste in her mouth and a desire not to repeat the experience. We will see.

Good news; Danni has just read this and recounts how much she enjoyed that trip. She even reminded me that we had chicken and chips at Linton Lock and said that she was really excited to sleep on the boat. I'm so pleased.

Chapter 7

Do you know; I wish my dad had involved me in just one adventure, although, he did lead by example, but it was not necessarily one that I have chosen to follow. I feel sure, that like most of us, he was a victim of his upbringing. He was from the generation who stuck at the same job forever. I admire the tenacity. Nice to think that a job could be there for life! I remember him proudly showing me a gold watch that the company he worked for, had given him, for twenty-five years of service. Some years before that, they had actually bought him a brand-new Triumph Speed Twin motorbike so that he could commute back and forth to work.

"Keep your nose to the grindstone lad," he would say.

He was a clever man, good with his hands. There were some pieces of furniture in their house that he had made; his woodwork was immaculate. He called himself an engineer, but my birth certificate records him as being a machine operator. I remember him building a television set, it had a tiny picture on a screen about twenty centimetres square which you viewed in very dark grey and white, with green in the background. No; don't be thinking of televisions as we know them today, this was when TV's first appeared and TV broadcasting in this country was in its infancy with just one channel, which was the BBC. Most people could only dream of owning one. Everybody had a radio. When it came to property, he never bought, he only rented, when rents were cheap. He never tried to improve himself in that way, I don't think he believed in it. But I never heard him swear, even when he accidentally put the garden fork right through his foot while he was digging. He was stuck in that certain Victorian mode of behaviour and strictness passed down to him by his father; that we seem to be losing in our society today. Some of those values would be worth keeping; some of them definitely not. Children were often a nuisance and were best kept out of site, or 'seen and not heard' as the saying goes. He expected food on the table when he got home from work and would kick up a stink if it wasn't. That stink would often turn into a blazing row between him and Bertha our stepmother. I can remember him storming into the house angrily demanding something from Bertha. Well; you know what you can do with that kind of chauvinism nowadays don't you. He had remarried after divorcing Ruby. The lady he chose for his second wife came to this country as a refugee trying to escape the madness of Adolf Hitler taking over Austria. I think my dad must have felt an affinity towards her, as our ancestral tree shows that his father originally came from Germany. Fancy that; some Germanic ancestry. I bet we are all a load of mongrels underneath really.

Chapter 8

Well, on my adventure with Danni. The lower door on Westwick Lock was really hard to open; I don't think the Canal and River Trust have improved it much to this day. Still, we managed, with one foot pushing on a nearby fence post; to help get some leverage. Then, out of the lock we went; feeling like veteran boaters, really pleased with ourselves and the journey we were undertaking.

The river level seemed to be even lower now, but it was hard to tell as we had never seen the river at its normal height. It was a pleasure to cruise passed Newby Hall, which was off to the right. On a nice summer's day, you might see a lot of visitors enjoying the gardens here and a little miniature train that carries people around the grounds; today the grounds looked deserted. About a half hour later, we found ourselves at Ox Close Lock. This is a pretty little lock that leads you onto The Ripon Canal which is the most northerly canal on the system and where the Ripon Racecourse Marina is, with our mooring to be. There is a flood gauge at the entrance to this lock. The bottom of the gauge is green and tells you that it is ok to go ahead; above that, the amber colour, reminds boaters to proceed with caution because of the raised water level; the top of the gauge is red, advising you to wait for the water to recede. The river level was just up to the red flood warning mark. Oops!

At Milby Lock and at Westwick the moorings are fixed, which is why they were underwater. Here at Ox Close though; there are floating pontoons below the lock, so mooring was no problem. Once again, we hardly had to open the lock paddles at all to get the water level before opening the gates and using the lock. Now we were on the last leg of our cruise; The Ripon Canal.

Cruising on a canal is not the same as a river because there is very little flow. It was late afternoon, in the distance ahead of us I could see a small red arched bridge over the waterway, a typical design that you can find on any canal. This bridge is called Renton's Bridge, it looked small. It is, in fact, the smallest bridge on this part of the canal system. As we approached it, we realised just how small it is. The headroom under the bridge must have been reduced by the increased height in the water level. Here was another bridge that looked like we might not fit under, our canopy was folded down, the windscreen was still standing up and despite my best efforts to steer through the bridge at the highest point, in the middle; I failed. A corner of the windscreen just caught the brick structure of the bridge. Danni and I both watched in horror and disbelief as the windscreen bent back some twelve inches and then pinged us off like a catapult. It was as if seeing a slow-motion film. I had seen the disaster coming and thrown the engine into reverse, but still, with our forward momentum, the boat kept advancing. It was just the weight of *Harnser* pushing us forward, that caused the screen to bend back, but miraculously it did not break.

Another half hour saw us tying the boat up to the pontoon we had rented in the marina at Ripon. The only casualty was a broken radio aerial. For us; the trip had been a bit of a legend. I think we were proud of ourselves for doing it, but glad it was over.

We abandoned *Harnser* for the car which we had left in the marina car park. It was good to be driving home. Looking at Danni sitting beside me as we went, gave my smile something to do. I often look at my family and know how grateful I am to have them. Ruth has been known to remind me how lucky I am, to be having a second go at it. She's right of course!

Chapter 9

After my dad had settled down with Bertha, his second wife, he came looking for me in Cornwall. When he found me, he took me back to London. He had already collected my sister, Irene, from the convent where Ruby had placed her. Now, suddenly, at age five years, I had a family. I can still remember that warm feeling of belonging, of realising that this was actually my own dad who was taking care of me. I had no concept of what a stepmother was, to me, at the time; Bertha was my mum. That is how it went; for a short while anyway.

This was 1948, not so long after war's end. There was still a lot of bomb damage to be seen. I have memories of that drive from Cornwall to London. My dad let me sit on his lap while he drove, so that I could pretend to be driving the car. I remember seeing the devastation; which could have been parts of London. The government had started a massive rebuilding program, because, with all the troops coming home after the war, housing was in short supply. A lot of homes must have been overcrowded. Dad had remarried. His new wife Bertha, had a twelve-year-old daughter, also, there was my sister, who had already been collected from the convent, plus, upstairs in their house, my grandma and grandad had a room; in what was a very small, three bedroom terraced property in Wembley with one toilet and no hot water. It had a bathroom, which had a large copper urn with a gas ring underneath it for heating water. Grandma and Grandad used the bathroom as their kitchen. They had a temporary wooden work surface on top of the bath with a small gas hob for cooking. Once a week, Sunday, the gas urn would be filled up and lit to heat water for a bath. It probably held enough water to fill the bath by about ten inches. The whole family would take it in turns to bathe in this water; first Grandad, then Grandma, then, my dad, then Bertha, then Georgina; Bertha's Daughter, then Irene and lastly; me. I bet you can't even imagine the smell of that water by the time I got into it and all that grey scum floating around on the surface of the now lukewarm water. Say one thing; they did used to save a cup or two of hot water for me to top the bath up with. I'm not sure if warm scum is nicer than cold though. Not that keen on baths anymore, thank heaven for the shower.

Infant school started at five years old, Irene was already attending school as she is a year older than me. As a young person, seeing a world full of adventure, I quite liked school to begin with, all I can remember doing is playing in the sandpit and making ice slides in the playground that first winter. Some of the kids were quite good at it. Mind you, it really wore out the soles of your shoes and that got me in trouble at home. As a five-year-old, I had no concept of shortages, of going out to work, earning money to feed and clothe a family. Not to mention keeping a roof over their heads.

Dad was the breadwinner, out to work at the crack of dawn and usually not back home till well after my bed time, so I hardly saw him and bed time was strictly adhered to. Bertha was what used to be called 'A Housewife', the little lady who stayed at home cleaning, looking after the kids, doing the laundry, the shopping and the cooking. We are all about 'equality' now, you are only tied to the kitchen sink if you choose to be, and we have all the mod-cons you can imagine. Back then, it was more or less compulsory, a woman's place was in the home and my god, how my dad stuck to that myth. I can still hear his voice demanding, "Where's my grub girl?" if his dinner wasn't on the table when he expected it, or "Why haven't I got a clean shirt?"

These were not pleasant requests, but orders from the man of the house.

Still, it was a special feeling, to be with one's very own family, how many of us, I wonder, take family for granted and it's not until things go pear-shaped that they realise what they have. I think things started to go pear-shaped for me after a year or so of living with Bertha.

Grandad had a stroke and died, he was only in his sixties, I hardly knew him, but I remember; he looked ancient; then again, I suppose that all older people look ancient to the young. You would hear him, upstairs, coughing his lungs up every morning. My dad had built me a bed in the corner, behind the front door, at the bottom of the stairs. From there, I might see Grandad wheeze his way down the stairs. Hard to imagine that he had been a world champion catch as catch can wrestler in his youth. No, I'm not kidding; He went to the USA to make a name for himself and apparently, made quite a good go of it. I have the American newspaper cuttings to prove it. His side of the family was the German connection, he was called Fred Gruhn. They had to change their name in the First World War when their bakery was burned down because of folk's prejudice and narrow mindedness. The name Gruhn sounded too German.

When Grandad had passed away, Bertha's attitude to Irene and I, seemed to harden, especially after she had a baby, which was a little boy. Irene and I were already starting to feel second best as Bertha had favour for her own now thirteen-year-old daughter and it sometimes felt like she resented us; she could be quite cruel and spiteful when displeased. She obviously had more time for her own offspring, Donald and Georgina. Postnatal depression and stress were probably her problems, though I cannot say that they were a recognised condition when I was a boy. Question is, was I pleased or sad, at the thought of having a little brother? Fact is; that I have never been close to him and was surprised in later years, when he tried to steal my first wife by offering her out and asking her what she was doing with a guy like me. Yes; Frances, my first wife, told me that.

One December day, not long after my Grandad's passing; Grandma slipped and fell while out buying tickets for Irene and I to go to the Christmas panto on ice at Wembley Stadium. She broke her hip. Not many people survived an accident like that. The ambulance men, bought her home from hospital, carried her upstairs to her bed and there she died a few days later.

I used to pop my head round her bedroom door to say good morning. No one knew that I had seen her when she passed away. It really gave me a fright, to see my Grandma lying in bed lifeless, a horrible yellowy grey colour. I felt that my last ally in the house had gone. She had known that Irene and I were not always treated kindly by Bertha and that we were often hungry. She would leave the crusts from her toast out, by her little stove in the bathroom for us to eat. Bertha had caught me eating some once and given me a hiding; then only fed me dry bread for the rest of that day. Irene shared some of her tea with me, when Bertha wasn't looking. Another time, she caught me getting a drink of water from the bath tap. I wonder if she got pleasure out of forcing me to drink glass after glass of water that Saturday morning, telling me that she was going to teach me not to steal water. Then I just brought it all up again along with the chopped peas and carrots she gave us for dinner. The reason that I remember it was a Saturday is because our Aunty Irene turned up to check if Irene and I were ok.

#

Aunty Irene was dad's sister, she was an independent lady who worked all her life and never married or had kids. She would arrive unannounced, usually on a Saturday, bringing with her some sweeties or an ice lolly for my sister and I. Bertha hated her coming round, I can see why. For instance; on that particular Saturday, Bertha had been having fun torturing me with glasses of water when Aunty Irene rang the doorbell. The thing that was really noticeable when any other person came on the scene was Bertha's demeanour. Butter wouldn't melt; all sweetness and light, the perfect mum having to cope with a troublesome child or two. Polite, kind, loving, considerate, wow! Where did this other person come from?

In 1994 I went to see my Aunty Irene; not having seen her since my childhood. She was an elderly lady then. We chatted and she confided to me that she had a good idea what was going on with Bertha and that is why she used to pop round sometimes; to make sure that Irene and I were alright. She told me that in the light of events that followed, she felt really guilty because she hadn't stepped in to try and do something.

Aunty Irene passed away shortly after that. I do hope that she was at peace with herself. She was undoubtedly a lovely person and had behaved in a manner that she thought best, at the time. Just like many of us; she was also a victim of her upbringing and circumstance. While talking to her on that last occasion I had tried to let her see how well things have finally turned out for me in adulthood and how resilient those early lessons have made me.

#

I kept the fact that I had seen my Granny dead in her bed as a little secret, because I was not supposed to go into her room or the bathroom, which she and Grandad had used as a kitchen. Yes, you can bet; as soon as Bertha discovered Granny had passed away, she locked Irene and I out of the house and closed all the curtains, which is what people used to do after a death in the house. Remember; 'Children seen and not heard.' In this case; whatever we were allowed to see or be part of, was censored. Ha!

I know my father must have missed his parents when they had gone. Though, I have never been sure if he didn't; in some way, blame Irene and I for the loss of his mother; as she had fallen while out buying a treat for us. It didn't take long for relations between Bertha and my sister and I, to deteriorate still further. Dad must have been working long hours, as he was never there to see fair play.

Having a baby brother made quite an impression on me, I don't know if it was a good one or a bad one. It did, however, cause me to sleepwalk from my bed behind the front door, into the living room, where his cot was. I was woken up with a start, not by Bertha and my dad fighting as quite often happened, but by the baby crying as I leaned over the side of his cot. I had no idea how I got there. Bertha was roused from her slumbers and came running downstairs to attend to him. Finding me beside Donald's cot; she must have been convinced that this six-year-old boy was a threat to her son. After that; she never allowed me any communication or interaction at all with Donald. In fact, I was almost completely banished from the house except for meal times and when Bertha needed things doing. Dad even made me a bed out in the shed above his work bench. I had to sleep out there for nearly three years till I was put in care.

Chapter 10

Back here in 2003, *Harnser* was quite a nice boat, she had been fairly well looked after but, unfortunately, some of the maintenance was of a poor standard. In your experience with a house, car or some other second hand item; you will probably have stumbled on a previous owner's lacking in this area yourself. Hey we can't all be perfect. Well; *Harnser* had been fitted with a new stainless-steel diesel tank, which must have been fashioned by a rabbit. Now I say that because I know rabbits can't weld and who ever made this tank could not weld. The very strong smell of diesel fuel was what alerted me to the problem when we returned to the boat. Remember I told you, we filled up with diesel before leaving York? Well; most of the forty gallons had leaked into *Harnser's* bilges. Sucking the remaining fuel out and removing the tank was fun; as was getting the fuel out of the bilges and cleaning up afterwards. An engineering company near me were good enough to re-weld the tank while installing proper strengthening bars inside it.

Harnser had automatic bilge pumps, which, luckily for us and the environment had not been maintained, so were out of order at the time; otherwise some of the fuel might have been pumped into the river.

Well; we didn't make as much use of *Harnser* as we would have liked to, that summer. Ruth was nursing in a care home, I had a full quota of music students to teach and the band I was working with were in high demand providing entertainment at functions and clubs; mostly on a Friday and Saturday night, just when our girls were off school for the weekend.

The next year 2004, we decided to cruise the boat down to York and use the same brokerage that we had bought her from to sell her. Danni would bring a school friend along to act as crew the first day, which would take us down to the marina at Boroughbridge, once there, I would stay on board for the night, Ruth would pick the girls up and take them home, then, in the morning, I would do the remainder of the trip on my own. Ruth would pick me up in York.

Next day, before setting off for York from the marina, I was having a conversation with a chap about boats. He seemed amazed that I was about to cruise down the river with such a large boat without any crew. It didn't feel like a big deal to me, there were only two locks to negotiate. Apparently, he knew someone who did it and forgot to loosen the mooring ropes in Linton Lock as the water went out of the pound.

"You have to pay attention and do not get distracted by talking to any one while you handle the locks". He warned.

Milby was the first lock I needed to negotiate on the way down to York. It's not a large lock; there is a drop of about two metres when you lower the water. Being near to Boroughbridge town centre it gets quite a few visitors. I expect you know that people who stand and watch boaters are nick named Gongoozlers. Well; there were quite a few Gongoozlers this day. Being watched while negotiating a lock can make you feel quite self-conscious and fairly important at the same time; a friendly chat is always welcome. Usually, the chat is about how to work the lock or maybe about the type of craft you have.

Have you guessed? Yes, I forgot the warning given to me by that chap in the marina before I left.

A very polite dog walker caught me in conversation as I was opening the lower sluice gates on the lock, to drain the water down. An interesting conversation started up about how heavy the lock gates are to open and close and what order you should open and close the paddles. I consider myself fairly fit; so, I nonchalantly began to explain in some depth, how using your weight and digging your heels in against the concrete blocks makes it pretty easy to move the gates.

I had my back to the lock and the boat while bragging, when the dog walker stopped me in midsentence by asking, "Should your boat be hanging like that?"

I turned to look at *Harnser* and was horrified to see that the water level had gone down almost to the bottom of her rudder. She was no longer floating, but hanging. You could see the propeller, which was now out of the water and the whole craft was miraculously suspended against the wall inside the lock by one mooring rope which I had attached to the centre mooring cleat. That's right; five tons of boat left hanging on one mooring rope.

More than a dozen people were stood watching. Now that; is when you feel stupid!

I don't know what the record speed of working a lock is, but I probably beat it. Like a maniac I closed the lower sluice gates and ran (or walked rather fast, because you shouldn't run around locks; neither did I want the Gongoozlers to think that I was panicking) to open the sluice gates at the top of the lock that let the water back into the chamber. Heart racing and out of breath from the exertion, gripping the lock key tightly in my hand, I watched anxiously as the water rose back up and slowly, all too slowly, re-floated *Harnser.*

Then I stood and smiled triumphantly at the Gongoozlers who were obviously pleased that I had averted a disaster and the other Gongoozlers who were looking disappointed at not having witnessed one.

Needless to say, the experience has caused me to learn a good lesson. Pay attention when someone is trying to give you some kindly advice. That trip was completed without any further mishaps and *Harnser* was delivered to the brokerage and subsequently sold.

Chapter 11

It would be wrong of me to say that all lessons in life are learnt with such ease, or that all mistakes can have such a happy outcome. The thing is; that all actions have a consequence which might be good or bad. The trick is to try and understand what the outcome of a given action might be. As we grow older; we hopefully learn better to deal with that conundrum, but when we are younger; well. Ignorance is bliss, so they say.

#

'Life with Bertha' soon became 'Hell with Bertha'. If either Irene or I caused her to have displeasure, it would lead to a tirade of verbal and physical abuse. We were both terrified of her. My sister would be the most careful not to upset her by being as quiet as a mouse and trying to do exactly as she was told, but Bertha would still find fault and launch into her, even breaking one of her front teeth on one occasion. I on the other hand; was fast learning to duck and dive.

Two of the things we had big issues with, were food and clothing. A lot of stuff was still in short supply or on ration, so I understand how you had to make good use of what you had and not waste anything. Today; in this country most of us have plenty of food and no shortage of things to wear. The shops are well stocked with everything you can think of. Back in the late 1940s and the 1950s things were a lot different. There were no supermarkets; just local speciality shops; Grocer, Butcher, Fishmonger, Greengrocer, if they didn't have what you wanted; you didn't trip off to another, you went without. I have often wondered if the shortage of food was a good excuse for Bertha to hand out a beating to Irene when her dinner plate wasn't quite empty. Fat and gristle on your plate needed to be eaten up, as did cold porridge. I became quite resourceful and would put any foodstuffs that Irene or I couldn't eat into my trouser pockets when Bertha wasn't looking, to dispose of down the road later. Unfortunately; one clothes washing day, which was always a Monday; Bertha discovered some of my gummed up trouser pockets. I got home from school to be confronted by an enraged stepmother, holding my short trousers in her hand with the pockets turned inside out. She proceeded to rub the food coated pockets viciously around my face, while handing out some verbal garbage in her nasty annoying Austrian accent.

Against this backdrop; now as an adult; I can understand the difficulties and frustrations of trying to keep a family clothed and fed. I have also observed that it is better to do things with kindness and love; I don't think Bertha knew the meaning of those words in relation to Irene and myself. Her true colours were showing through; as was her resentment of us.

There was no love lost between my stepmother and me, as you can imagine, but I will be careful not to only mention Bertha's shortcomings; she was, in fact, a master of all things domestic. This type of woman was perfectly suited to a man like my dad; who had no interest in domesticity or his kids, but only went out to earn the money to keep a roof over his family's head. Then when he eventually arrived home; he would expect everything to be just as he would like it. There would be a scene if it wasn't. She had her job, he had his.

Unlike my dad, who taught me nothing, Bertha was committed to teaching us everything she could, from scrubbing tiled floors and polishing furniture to darning wool socks, knitting, jam making, window cleaning, gardening, washing, ironing, the list must have included everything domestic and practical that needs to be done to run a household. She was the pernicketiest person you could imagine. Most of the time, it was impossible to please her. I don't resent her; or that time in my life. I have often been glad of things that she showed me. Irene and I spent our sixth, seventh, eighth and ninth years with Bertha. Just about four years, most of it in fear of what she would do to us next, but we did learn a lot of useful things from her.

Do you remember I told you how I ended up having to sleep out in the shed? Well; next door's garden had an apple tree in it with a wonderful crop of juicy apples that year. How many of you have never been scrumping? Let me tell you, when I was left alone in that shed at night with a hungry belly, the temptation was too great. Out I would creep, when all was quiet, over the fence and gather a midnight feast.

It had to happen didn't it; I was seen by a neighbour, who tittle tattled over the garden fence about this young boy she had seen climbing into next door's garden in his pyjamas while she was putting the cat out about eleven o'clock one night and robbing apples from poor old Mrs Taylor's tree.

Well, that scandal got back to Bertha, who promptly had dad fit a lock on the shed door to secure me in at night. Little did Bertha realise that, being a small lad, I could easily squeeze out of the window. Which is what I did, but; I was seen again. Yes, this ghostly young boy climbing into next door's garden in his pyjamas in the middle of the night was again the subject of chatter over those garden fences.

Bertha's next ploy was of course to have my dad nail the window shut. I cannot imagine how she coerced him into locking me out there in the first place. All I can think is that she refused him sex unless he did as she asked. The reason I have come to that conclusion, is that when I was thirteen and had been sent home for a trial period; I heard him banging on her bedroom door one night, demanding to have reinstatement of his conjugal rights. I remember he was shouting through the door, "Open up girl, I demand reinstatement of my conjugal rights".

I had no idea what that meant at the time, ha! ha! Anyway, as far as I was aware, she ignored him; poor fellow.

Let me get back to the point that I was leading up to. Being locked in the shed with no access to a toilet at night caused me a problem. When I could come and go as I pleased, I used to nip out and pee in the garden, but now, that was not possible, as I was locked in. So, where could I do it? In one of those handy bottles that are behind the door, of course! Those were dad's beer bottles which he used to save up each week by storing them in the shed. Bottles were important, because you had to leave a three-penny deposit on each one when purchasing beer or soft drinks to take home. Take the bottles back, get your deposit back. We had never heard of bottles made out of plastic that you just threw away, although apparently; they were first commercially introduced in 1947 but were very expensive. Anyway, this particular night, I had to go to toilet, so I did it in one of those beer bottles... Bertha found it!

When she had finished beating me, she made me drink it... and wash the bottle out as well. Yes, it would have been wrong to leave it smelling of pee!

Another source of conflict arose with our stepmother when I was seven. She insisted that we hurry home from school and do not dawdle. Bertha seemed to like the word 'dawdle', because she used it often. The walk home from school was probably less than a mile. There were a few occasions when we were later home than she would have liked. Well; we were kids. Sometimes we would just be late out of class; other times we were probably mucking about with other kids or even dawdling! You can understand her being concerned. The first couple of times it was a verbal telling off; then it became a beating. It didn't matter what excuse you gave; you were a liar and apparently; she could see it written all over your face. (Bertha always said that when she thought she'd caught you doing something and you denied it.) At that time, most parents didn't shuttle their kids back and forth to school. Hardly any families had a car. We used to walk everywhere or get the bus; if we had the money. I'm not sure why Bertha didn't come to meet us from school if she was so concerned. It didn't seem to bother her how long it took us to get to school, or indeed, if we even did get to school. Funny old world isn't it?

The trip to school had originally been supervised by Georgina, our step sister, but she was much older than Irene and I and was soon attending a big school somewhere else. She left home quite young having completed a 'shorthand typing' course and got herself a job in Canada. I think she must have struggled with the tension that so often existed in the house.

Irene somehow learnt the lesson about not dawdling quite quickly; I never did; which usually meant a battering from Bertha when I finally did arrive home from school. Her logic was that if Irene got home by four; why couldn't I? Irene, did in fact learn how to keep on the right side of Bertha most of the time. I can only imagine that the regime in a convent would have been pretty strict, so I guess she was used to towing the line.

Things came to a head for me one day when, on the way home, I reached the main road that had to be crossed before going into Sylvia Gardens where we lived. Then, looking up at the clock above the off licence, which was on the corner, I could see that it was one minute past four. Now; this is a bit like the Cinderella story, except that Cinder's deadline was twelve o'clock; mine was four o'clock. One minute past four and Bertha would go into her Jekyll and Hyde routine. That afternoon after school, when I looked at that clock; I was too scared of Bertha to go on home. Besides; the sun was shining; other kids were out playing, so I didn't go home.

I was seven years old, the first time I stayed out. It wasn't my intention to run away, just to keep away from Bertha and save myself a beating. I remember bumping into another lad from school who was with his mum. She was nice enough to take me home with them and give me tea. Then the kid and I played in their garden till it was his bedtime, when his mum told me to "Run along home now."

I don't think that kid or his mum, had any idea of my predicament. I contrived to go home with him quite a few times. He became the friend I would latch on to after school, knowing as I now did, that his mum would make me welcome. I have a fond memory of being at his house one summer evening and his mum filling the large tin bath with water outside on their porch for us to mess about in.

That particular afternoon after school, like many others, ended up with me simply roaming the streets. My dad would tour those streets on his pushbike later in the evening, when he'd finished work, looking for me. Sometimes he would find me, put me on the crossbar of the bicycle and pedal me home. I can still hear his heavy breathing in my ear, as I balanced there hanging on to the handlebars. Other times he wouldn't find me at all and I would be too scared to go home; or was it just a sense of adventure that made me stay out. I usually found something to eat and somewhere to sleep. I knew of an old car that was often left unlocked, it actually had a travel blanket on the back seat and that back seat smelt of leather as I laid on it. I was still freezing cold on an endless winter night though. Then there was a derelict upturned rowing boat with a hole in the bottom, lying on some rough ground in the scout club yard. I had seen it when I was allowed to go to the cubs. You had to climb a high fence to get to it, but you were certain not to get discovered in there. I woke up several times with creepy crawlies on me; that was nasty. I remember, thinking how it would be alright with the new mackintosh Bertha had bought me, which was a waterproof one made from some new material they called plastic. The 'mac' got torn when I climbed the fence and filthy from the ground under the boat, then subsequently, when I was back at home, there was hell on with Bertha as she had to throw it away.

One evening I had insisted to Bertha that we be allowed to stay up late in order to see our dad when he got home from work. I didn't tell her that I wanted to report her terrible treatment of Irene and I to him. When I did tell dad, what was going on; Bertha of course, denied it, so he asked Irene if it was true. To my surprise, Irene denied it as well, saying, "No daddy it isn't true, he's telling lies."

Irene was of course terrified of reprisals from our stepmother, her denial of the truth only fuelling my dad's conviction that I had made it up as an excuse for not returning home. I knew it at the time, but Irene has come clean to me in later years. One thing I realised was that Bertha would not lay a finger on us if dad was around. That was all part of her Jekyll and Hyde life. My dad would give me a hiding when he got me home at night, but it was what you might call a tame hiding, with a belt across my backside. It wasn't a patch on Bertha's sadistic beatings. I hated it, but I could live with the difference.

I would like to tell you more about those times later, but you must be wondering what happened to our boating adventures after we sold *Harnser* in 2004.

Chapter 12

Having a boat, a caravan or a mobile home can be like having a 'White Elephant' if you don't use it enough. There you have what could be a massive responsibility just sitting unused for much of the year. This is not so bad if it isn't costing you a fortune to keep. You could have a caravan or motorhome sitting on your driveway, that won't cost anything, except maybe, for road tax and insurance. But a boat; well, the fact is that mooring up in most marinas is going to be costly, so it was lucky for us, there is a boat club with its own marina that we were able to join.

We gained membership to a boat club in Ripon in 2004. Here you have a lot of boaters, all joining together to enjoy cruising the rivers and canals, while also having the pleasure of a great social scene and knowledge sharing. All running of the club is carried out by its members; this self-help ethos means that we all benefit from affordable moorings. The first order of business on joining the club was to buy another cruiser. With so many boats all in one place there was bound to be a few for sale.

A thirty one foot Project cruiser called *Ocean Magic* was our choice. She had been lifted out of the water for winter refurbishment and looked in good shape. A solid cabin had been added on the stern where the canopy would normally be. She had twin diesel engines and two outdrives. My thinking was that the two engines would give you double security while on the river; after all, it is most unlikely that they would both break down together. If one failed; you would still have the other engine to limp along with. The two outdrives would make it easier for a novice like me to steer. I have always been an optimist.

When that summer half term came, we were ready to set off on our new boat for a few days. The girls helped Ruth and I load everything aboard. Misty, our tricolour border collie, had to be safely put aboard as well. (On later trips, we even took our two guinea pigs in their cage.) It was a lovely bright late May afternoon when we set off for Boroughbridge, where we would spend our first night aboard *Ocean Magic*, although, we did have a couple of trial nights in the marina. Next day, we would cruise on down to York, moor up in Museum Gardens, where most of the boat people moor and go exploring the city.

Westwick Lock was behind us when the port engine started to stutter. It didn't stop completely, it just sounded really unhealthy for a while. Then; as if by magic, it carried on running normally. We made it to Boroughbridge by about five o'clock. Moored up and had a walk around the town. The fish and chips smelt inviting at one of the pubs, so we went in and had some for our tea. I noticed that they had live music on a Saturday night. That was my cue to chat the landlord up into letting me do a gig there with my band one Saturday in August; which led to several other gigs, but unfortunately, like so many other pubs, this one closed down the next year. I guess nothing stays the same, it doesn't seem so long ago, since pub culture meant that we all stood round a piano at the 'local' on a Saturday night, singing songs together; songs that everybody knew. Smoke filled rooms, (glad they've gone) inebriated folk staggering home; yes, and some of them driving home as well. Necessary rules from our government have changed all that. There have been many social fashions and changes in recent years that have also had a devastating effect on our pub culture.

We spent a comfy night on the *Magic* at Boroughbridge. In the morning after breakfast, we set off towards York. Got through Milby Lock with ease, headed on down towards Linton Lock. An hour or so into the cruise to Linton, that port engine started to stutter again; then died. Oh well! We still had the starboard motor and it was doing fine, for a while. Steering was a bit one sided, having only one propeller, but we were managing ok till the starboard engine chugged to a disappointing stop, leaving us drifting on the current for a minute or two. I was standing at the tiller in a dazed state, trying to get an engine restarted. How could both engines possibly let us down on the same trip? The river looked deserted of other boaters, which was surprising, as the day was really calm and pretty. We weren't too far from Linton Lock, the current pushing us, was heading over the weir that goes around the lock cut. That rang the alarm bells! You should have seen Ruth and I leaning over the side of the boat, trying to row her into to the bank with pots from the galley. It's all we had, but we got the *Magic* close enough to the trees to allow us to pull her in and moor up; time to look at those engines.

Out came the tools and diesel manuals we keep aboard. I took a quick look up the river to see if any other boaters were about who might be able to help. There was a small craft heading down the river towards us, so we hailed and shouted out to them. On catching their attention, we encouraged them to steer over to us. They were an elderly couple; very amicable, the chap looked quite overweight and was wheezing heavily, he was obviously poorly. It turned out that he had just had a triple heart bypass and this was his first venture out. Still, he was up for throwing us a line and towing us into the Linton Lock cut, so we could moor up safely to work on the engines. This indeed they did. The couple's names were Paul and Mary; we could see the effort caused him a great deal of distress. He was sweating profusely when we got into Linton and untied his line from our boat. We all went into the pub for refreshments. Then, we thanked them for their kindness, helped them through the lock and away they went down river. I do hope that he was alright.

Ruth sent a text to her brother, asking if he would drive down from Bedale and pick her, the girls and our dog up to take them home. I stayed with the boat to repair the engines.

The problem was lack of maintenance. Both filters were thick with debris. We only learnt later, that the previous owner had never actually cruised the boat, despite owning it for some years. I stayed at Linton for two days working on the engines and then only managed to limp back to Ripon on one of them. Diesels can be difficult to restart sometimes after changing fuel filters, especially if you get air into the fuel injection system. I needed a stronger battery and someone with more knowledge to fire up that second engine. I knew I would find them at the club. That was where a chap showed me how to bleed air out of the system, it was so simple.

We did eventually manage several trips to York down the River on *Ocean Magic*. The most serious other incident was probably when Misty, our border collie, having an upset tummy, trailed sloppy poo all around the decks while we weren't looking. (I suppose you didn't want to know that.) It was quite embarrassing; we were moored up alongside other boaters with lots of Gongoozlers watching at Museum Gardens as we attempted to swab the decks clean. Eeuk! We got Misty when she was a puppy; she lived for seventeen years, which I'm told is very good for a border collie.

Chapter 13

As far as I am aware, my father never called the police if I didn't go home after school. Can you imagine that today? Social care must have been in its infancy in the early fifties, or asleep; what's another kid or two getting a beating, then running away from home? I must have occasionally led my parents a merry song and dance. Interestingly; no one batted an eyelid at an eight-year-old kid, standing in the lobby of The Harrow Tavern pub at ten o'clock in the evening singing for money. There would always be at least one pub leaver give me a few coppers. When I had sixpence, I would be straight over to the chip shop, which wasn't open every night, for a bag of chips. Another good place to go for some supper, proved to be a bakery just off Wembley High Street. There was a useful back door which was often left open. I found it by following the irresistible smell of bread floating through the town at about three o'clock one morning. Getting a drink was never a problem, as apart from the Express Dairy's milk floats, there was always a drinking water fountain to be found by climbing over the gates to get into the park which were locked shut at night by a Park Keeper.

I remember there were some Friday evenings when my father didn't manage to find me, which resulted in me staying out the whole weekend. I slept rough, Friday, Saturday and Sunday night. You spend a lot of the waking day time waiting for some other normal kids to come out to play in the park, so that you have some company. I have to tell you though; on one of those Saturday nights I managed to climb over the fence at Wembley Stadium to watch the speedway. You could smell the 'Castrol R' oil that the motorbike engines used to burn and hear those engines revving when you were outside the stadium. Listening to the roar of the spectators from outside the stadium was like a magnet. Some of the kids at school used to brag about how they had been to speedway with their dads.

Did my dad lie awake all night worrying about me? How did he know that I would always go to school the next school day? That's where he would come looking for me. When I arrived at Monks Park School after roaming the streets and sleeping rough, can you picture what a mess I must have been in? Still, to my knowledge, no one contacted any social welfare department. My dad would turn up at some point in the morning, take me home and clean me up. What do you suppose he told the teacher?

Once home, I would also be given a hiding and then locked in the shed. On one of those occasions, I was so tired after my weekend's adventure, that I was dizzy and hallucinating. I have never been high on drugs, but I imagine it would be like that. There, locked in the gloomy shed, a spider on that cobweb in the corner was in fact a monster with eight legs and huge eyes. Every little speck of dust and dirt was alive and looked like a predator of some kind, nothing looked as it should it was horrendous, I buried my head into the blanket and eventually exhaustion took over, allowing me to sleep.

Yes; I would always go to school; I have no idea why. I can't say I had a thirst for knowledge at the time or for school discipline. I can't even say that I had lots of friends there. Having to wear Georgina's hand me down long blue knickers which hung out from under my short trousers, had made me a source of ridicule on more than one occasion. As had the hand-me-down shoes with toes cut out so that my feet would fit in to them; and that was in the winter. Getting chilblains was a regular occurrence when the weather turned cold. One year I even got frost bite in all my toes. You remember I told you how Bertha was a capable woman; well, she knew exactly how to deal with frostbite. You get a sharp knife and cut off all the affected toe parts. Oh! There's no pain, as the frost has killed all the flesh off. Luckily, it was only the pads of my toes and they grew back again.

#

There was one particular boy at school, much older than me who I got involved with. His name was David Wise. He had a reputation for always being in trouble. I was very wary of him, but he was the only kid who would be allowed to stay out late; most of the other kids having to go home around seven or eight o'clock. One particular afternoon that I stayed away from home was the year I was going to be ten years old at the end of July. It was the afternoon we broke up for school summer holidays. David Wise was fifteen that year and had finished school for good. He was on the flat roof of the junior school showing off. Several of the teachers were trying to get him down from the roof; it was quite a show and lots of us stayed to watch. When he did eventually climb down, he proceeded to hand the teachers a ton of abuse and ran off down the road. Of course, all of that nonsense made me late home, so when I arrived at the crossing by the off licence near Sylvia Gardens, it was fifteen minutes past four. No going home to face Bertha for me. I did what I always did when not going home; I went to the park.

Later on, that evening I had made my way up to Wembley and ran into David Wise. He was with two other older boys. I hung around with the three of them getting into various bits of mischief. It wasn't long before the streets were empty and everything was closed. In those days, high streets became like ghost towns at night. Pubs closed at ten-thirty and everyone went home. Come about midnight, the only car you might see would probably be a police car and the only pedestrian was probably a bobby on the beat.

Well, it happened that the four of us found ourselves in a back alley behind some shops, one of which was a restaurant called 'The Cherry Tree'. These three older lads must have been intending to go there and I had just followed on. Anyway, they wanted to break into this restaurant but none of them was small enough to get through the little transom window which had been left open. They promised me some ice cream if I would climb in and open the door for them. Ice cream sounded good on a warm summer night, so I clambered in, it was easy. I let them in the door, got myself an ice cream and a bottle of lemonade then made off. I went and sat on a grass railway embankment nearby that overlooked the end of Wembley High Street. David Wise joined me a bit later, bragging about how him and his mates had just ransacked the restaurant.

There we were, enjoying our spoils at about two o'clock in the morning, when a police man walking the beat on the street below, saw us, scrambled up the embankment and collared me before I could make a getaway. David Wise made off, but both he and the other two lads were caught later. This bit of mischief naturally came up before the Magistrates, which is when the goings-on at Sylvia Gardens, were bought to the attention of the authorities.

As a result of these events; I was placed under the care and protection of the Middlesex County Council. I have done much research and managed to locate copies of court files and care records from the London Archives dating back to 1954. It seems that a welfare officer was sent round to see and interview Bertha. His report states that he found her to be a competent housewife and mother, who kept an immaculate house and that I must have 'Romanced' the whole saga of the mistreatment handed out by her. Lucky for me, having got all of their reports, the magistrates thought differently. It seems that there was a shortage of places in children's homes at the time; which was even luckier for me, because I was found a place in a boarding school out in the country. My sister, Irene, on the other hand, was not put in care, but was sent to live with dad's older sister and her husband in Finchley.

St Christopher's was a small, mixed private prep school run by a middle-aged spinster lady called Miss Ely. The only bad thing about the school was her brother Mr Ely, who was a bit of a sadist when it came to boxing, always insisting that best friends put the gloves on and try to knock each other's brains out in the ring. He would dance around the combatants shouting and shadow boxing while trying to egg them on.

"Go on bash him", or "Now lad, get one in there."

He was an ex-RAF man who was also a stickler for discipline.

Thankfully, he was only around part time. Miss Ely ran a very upper-class school. Elocution, Latin and music lessons were all on the timetable. Her clientele included the American ambassador's children and a lord's son. Sunday mornings, we would all put on our best uniforms and walk in two's neatly down the quiet country lane in Little Missenden, Buckinghamshire, to attend the local church service. Some Sunday afternoons, parents would visit. There would be one or two Rolls Royce, an American car, and a couple of other fancy vehicles in the driveway. My dad came a few times, on a motorbike. I was the envy of the other kids because I got to ride on the back of it. One time, I persuaded him to give my friend David Cole a ride. Now there's a thing; no crash helmets and taking a boy you don't even know on the pillion of your motorbike. No; it wasn't wrong; that's the way things were back in 1955. I think it's called trust or maybe stupidity, depending on your leaning.

I found my first girlfriend at St Christopher's when I was about eleven. Her name was Rosalyn. She had long blonde hair and was taller than me. I had only seen her coming and going down the narrow corridor outside the dining room. I don't know what came over me. One day I just leaned up and kissed her on the cheek as we passed each other. I could hear all her friends giggling as I retreated on down the corridor to the boot room feeling very foolish. Hey; it turned out that she fancied me too. We spent the next few weeks mooning around together, not knowing what to say to each other half the time or what we were supposed to be doing. Anyway, when Rosalyn started trying to avoid me, I knew the game was up. Ahh! Young love eh?!

Reading the old records, I was interested to notice that St Christopher's probably only took me in reluctantly. At different times in my three years there, Miss Ely has made notes on whether or not I was shaping up. At one point she wrote about how she was expecting to make a grammar school boy of me yet. I don't regret never becoming a grammar school boy; sorry if I let her down, but I am eternally grateful for the chance of a place at St Christopher's, as for me it was a life saver and an amazing awakening to the value of standards in life, to music and to learning.

When the school holidays came, all the other children went back to their own homes. I was sent to a wonderful little children's home in Hanwell, just outside London, as I was not permitted back home to Sylvia Gardens. There were eight boys in the home, which was run by a lovely lady called Mrs Bunford. The boys called her Aunty Bunford. She had the look of someone from the Victorian era who you would expect to be very motherly and always in the kitchen. Not tall, or fat but round and homely looking. I got on well with the lads there. I think, because they were all really streetwise and I could easily associate with the kinds of things they got up to, which was quite different from the middle-class children at boarding school, who I loved, but they had a tameness about them. I can only say how great it was to have such variation in my life.

Many years later, when I was thirty, sitting in a beer garden in Perth, Western Australia, with my first wife and our children, a chap kept staring at me from another table. It was starting to annoy me, when he came over to us, smiled and said, "Aunty Bunford". Can you believe, he remembered me from all those years ago and we were on the other side of the world? His name was Peter; I hadn't recognised him, as he had changed so much in adulthood, but there was no mistaking the name 'Aunty Bunford'.

I was sad to leave St Christopher's at thirteen years of age. It was a prep school and at that stage, most of the kids went on to grammar school. Apparently, I had failed my eleven-plus by just one mark, so no grammar school for me. I was, however, sent home to Sylvia Gardens for a 'Trial Period' of six months. Having to go back there filled me with fear and trepidation. I can remember arriving at Marylebone Station with my suitcase, expecting to be met by my welfare officer and wondering if I wouldn't just go somewhere else; anywhere but to see Bertha.

Well, there you go. I was obviously wrong about that. Bertha must have been warned off or she was scared of me, as at thirteen I was a bigger boy now.

Bertha seemed to me to have shrunk as she was much shorter than I remembered and was completely indifferent to me. It felt as if her whole mode of behaviour was a put on act. This was just not the

Bertha we knew before. Still; life carried on. I was sent to Copeland Secondary Modern School. This was a huge, school with umpteen hundreds of pupils. There were over forty pupils in just one class, which was significantly different from St Christopher's, which only had about forty pupils in the whole school. At St Christopher's I'd had piano lessons which took me right up to grade six. At Copeland, they didn't even have a music lesson at that time.

I soon got to know some local lads who all had bicycles, but unfortunately, I didn't. It turned out though, that there were a lot of old disused cycles in a shed at the local council flats. One of these young men showed them to me, assuring me that no one owned any of them. There were indeed a great number of bicycles, just piled in the shed, most of which were in a sorry state, with parts missing. Without thinking, I sorted out one of these bikes, one that had unusual, red walled tyres, it was just as rusty and neglected as all the others, but this one seemed to be complete. When my dad asked where it came from, he seemed satisfied with my reply that it was one someone had thrown out. Then I cleaned it up and made it rideable again. Most days, for about two weeks, I rode it around the streets with the other lads. One day, a man stepped off the pavement as I was riding past him and stopped me. Apparently, this bike belonged to his daughter, who had gone abroad. He knew the bike by its red tyres. I was hauled before the magistrates for theft of a bicycle. Stealing a bicycle had been the last thing on my mind, though admittedly, it was naïve of me not to have asked around to check if anyone actually still wanted the bike. Enthusiasm probably got the better of me. (Reading the records, I see that four other boys were also in court.) Having been home for only about two months and not being too happy there; I was glad to be put back into care. That is when they sent me to Denham Court; which I have already told you about.

Sometimes I wonder if we don't affect what happens to us by the way we think. More than once in my life, coincidences and events have led me to believe that. On the other hand, maybe we all just have an angel.

Chapter 14

Before I tell you about another boat venture, you are going to learn about 'Old Man Chappell'. Remember him? He was the House Father at Denham Court. Both he and Mr Hill were seldom on duty at the same time. It was usually one or the other, they took it in turns. Mr Chappell was an ex-naval man who could be firm, but was often more forgiving than Mr Hill. As a result, I think the boys preferred it when he was on duty. Being a smaller man than Mr Hill and a lot softer spoken was probably what enamoured him most to the boys. He had black hair that was always greased back and a very ruddy complexion.

Everything worked to a time table at Denham, which meant that we had a rotor telling each of us what duties we had to do and when. For instance; when it was our turn to wash up, peel the potatoes (for about 40 boys) or when it was our bath night.

If you weren't first in the bath, you had to wait your turn as there were only four baths, which were all set side by side with no privacy screens between them. One day, Mr Chappell, on seeing me standing, shivering at the back of the queue for a bath, told me to use his personal bath, down the corridor in his quarters. I was delighted, not so much to leave the queue, as thinking that I must be on his good side.

I was in his bath, washing myself, when he came in to check my progress. He seemed pleased with me for getting on with it and then started to help me wash. I didn't think anything of at first as he was the master in charge and he had a kindly nature. He had me stand up and got more ambitious with his washing efforts, concentrating more on my private parts. He finished off his work and told me that we would keep it a secret; me using his bath as the other lads would be jealous.

Well, as you might guess, I had become more streetwise than innocent, so I thought I had a good notion of what 'Old Man Chappell' was about. In reality, I had no concept of his depravity. A couple of weeks later, he told me to use his bath again; it was more of an instruction than a request. If you were told to do something, you didn't refuse; you just got on with it. Then; just like the last time he came in to the bathroom on pretence of making sure I was washing properly (you know, 'Behind the ears'). He took the flannel to help me make a better job of it and of course, he got more familiar with what he did; eventually dropping his own trousers and trying to get me to wash his privates, which was very distressing. Still, despite him being the adult in charge, I did manage to keep the situation under some control by squeezing my buttocks together really tightly so that his penis could only get between my legs when he tried to bugger me. I won't go into all the sordid details of what he did or tried to do, just to let you know, that on seeing how much he was upsetting me; he tried to comfort me by asking if there were any toys or sweets I would like him to buy me. I told him that I collected Meccano. He offered to buy some bits for my set and subsequently he did buy me a clockwork motor kit and some other parts. Being on the promise of a gift from the experience and then finally actually getting one, I felt in no position to tell anyone else about it, which worried me greatly, as I had no idea when he might tell me to use his bath again.

I saw him send one of the other boys down to his bathroom one evening and I knew what was going on. In a weird sort of way, that made me feel rejected, yet I was glad it wasn't me and I found myself perversely wondering if the other lad had been before and if he enjoyed the attentions of 'Old Man Chappell'.

Thankfully; somehow, 'Old Man Chappell' was caught. I have no idea who told on him or how he was found out. It turned out that there were four of us lads who were his victims. We were taken to give evidence against him at Warwick Crown Court. That in itself is a story worth telling.

#

When the authorities took us to court, we weren't briefed in any way That is to say, we had no idea of the seriousness of the occasion. I don't think any of us really understood what was going on except that 'Old Man Chappell' had been found out. The four of us were shut in a little room on our own and summoned, one at a time through a door, which led to what proved to be a witness box, where we were stood facing a court room full of unfamiliar stern faces some of whom were wearing long white wigs. While it is true that a court room may not have been that unfamiliar to me, having been in a juvenile court not so long before, a Crown Court is a whole different ball game. There we were, having to swear on a Bible and being asked so many embarrassing questions; then having someone else ask you more questions, all the time implying that you might be lying, was certainly a trial.

When the youngest of the four of us, came back into the room where we were waiting, he was in floods of tears. None of the adults seemed to care; he was just bundled back into the room without a word of sympathy. Between us, we had been trying to make light of the situation, it always being better to laugh than to cry in difficult times. It turned out that this young chap must have suffered worse than the rest of us at the hands of Mr Chappell, as he had actually been buggered by him. None of us knew what the word 'bugger' meant at the time and this kid was partially upset because he thought that no one in the court had understood what he meant when he said that Mr Chappell had stuck his dick up his backside. To make matters worse though; on hearing this lad tell us what happened to him, Ginger Wolacott began running around the room hysterically shouting to the other two of us in turn, "He bummed him Rod, He bummed him Lambo!"

This of course had us cracking up with laughter and only served to upset the poor kid even more.

No one told us how the trial ended. When we were back at Denham Court after the trial, we were misinformed that Mr Chappell had been sent back to the navy; the actual result of the proceedings was kept secret from us. Of course, common sense told me that this couldn't be true, but for sixty years, I have been under this wrong impression. We weren't even told where that trial was held. I was hoping to find the correct answer in my care records if and when I found them. Well; my care records weren't too hard to find and I would like to express my gratitude to all those people from various archives who helped me to locate them.

A record of a child's time in care usually contains every detail of their lives; all their trials and tribulations, as well as the responses to certain situations by the carers. My care record is no exception. Eight years of being in the care system had been carefully written down in black and white; with comments about my behaviour; whether it was good or bad and about what my carers thought of me etcetera, etcetera, but there is not a single word about that episode with Mr Chappell. None! I was beginning to think the whole thing was a product of my imagination. Why do you suppose such a traumatic event was kept secret? You don't suppose that it was to save the council from embarrassment, do you??

So; the truth of what happened to Mr Chappell remained a closed book. I had to dig around in more archives only to discover that this particular trial had been hidden away in a locked file at the records office for a hundred years. There doesn't appear to be a good reason for that, so much for 'Freedom of Information'. I was denied access to those court files.

However, Lady Luck smiled on me again, as one of the clerks at the records office, privately emailed me details of just how to obtain access to them. Apparently; you can only access these files if the person concerned has died and you can produce a death certificate. So, the challenge was to find out what had become of Mr Chappell. That is exactly what I did and two weeks later, I presented the archives with a copy of his death certificate, on the correct application form of course.

Bet your busting to know what happened to 'Old Man Chappell'. Well, he got sixteen years in prison. Four years for each of us. Finally, I can lay that to rest.

Yes, I have claimed compensation, not just for what Chappell did, but for the complete lack of concern shown by our carers the Middlesex County Council, who as a matter of fact were disbanded in 1965 to become the Greater London Council.

Chapter 15

In 2003 when I was at the boat yard looking over *Harnser*, I noticed there were a lot of other vessels standing around that looked like they could do with a bit of TLC. I mentioned this to Warren the salesman, he said,

"They are mostly part exchanges that we will sell off cheap to get rid of them."

It occurred to me that there might be some wheeling and dealing to be done here. If one were to spend a bit of time repairing any minor faults, then cleaning and polishing a boat, it could be sold for a better price. On discussing this with Warren, we came to an agreement. He would sell me a boat cheap; I would fix it up; then he would sell it on for a better price, we would share the profit. A key addition to the deal was that the boat being worked on could stay in the yard without incurring any rental charge. This was important, as it meant I wouldn't incur any costs except for materials and car fuel coming and going to the yard.

I got stuck in. The arrangement worked quite well for more than half a dozen boats. I would drive down to York most days, weather permitting and spend time doing up boats. The work was mostly cleaning and polishing to make a craft look pretty again. None of the cruisers were as big as *Harnser*, we didn't make huge amounts of profit, but it was fun to do and gave me motivation. Warren always made a special effort to get a quick sale on whatever boat I had just done up. This enterprise went on for about six months before the bubble burst.

One day when I arrived at the yard there was a new man in charge who knew nothing of the situation. Warren had got another job and moved on without giving me any warning; the new yard man had no interest in carrying on with any wheeling and dealing. He also wanted to charge me rent for boat space, which didn't make the effort worthwhile. You can never tell how long the craft might stand there before being sold. None of that would have been a problem as I could have just walked away except that Warren had just sold me a rather expensive marine ply boat. He had sung the praises of this twin-engine cruiser so much that he convinced me it would be a good project for our next venture.

Well, obviously I was being royally ripped off. I am not one to shy away from a challenge. Every week that boat stood there was going to cost me money and how long would it take the salesman to sell her when I had finished the clean up? Would he even try?

On further investigation of this marine ply cruiser I found some serious wood rot in more than one place that had been cleverly hidden beneath layers of paint. This led me to the conclusion that I was unlikely to get my money back on this boat at all, in fact it looked like I might lose quite a bit. The new yard man proved to be most unhelpful even wanting to charge me for use of the electric point, which had been part of the deal with Warren.

I decided the only way to come out of this with a shirt still on my back was to break the boat up for parts. Just the two good engines with perfect outdrives would fetch enough to cover my original investment. The galley had a good cooker, fridge and a sink with nice brass taps. There was a water pump, a shower pump, I've kept the huge bilge pump, it has been really useful. When you start looking around with the intention of breaking for parts, a cruiser like this has mountains of good chandlery that will all sell on eBay along with the rest of the bits and pieces. I knew very well that the shell of the hull would be left on the hard standing; my plan was to abandon it there. Did I hear you mutter naughty, naughty! It wasn't really naughty; it's called 'Self Preservation'.

This needed careful planning, the new boat salesman was never going to stand for me breaking a boat up in the yard; let alone leaving the carcass for him to dispose of. I had noticed that the chap didn't arrive for work till late each morning; so, I got there early with my tools and chain saw. I ended up spending the whole of the first day discreetly taking everything apart, ready for removal from the hull. The engines were ready to lift out, the outdrives dismantled, even some of the windows had been unbolted pending their removal as I was sure someone would want to buy them.

The next morning, I went back to the boatyard with a friend of mine who runs a builder's yard. His lorry has one of those cranes on the back for lifting heavy building materials on to site; we would need the crane to lift the engines out of the hull. By midday when the yard man turned up, we had the lorry loaded with everything resalable. When he saw what was happening, the look on his face was epic. We were just getting into the lorry to set off home; I couldn't stop myself from smiling at the situation.

I am happy to tell you that every piece of chandlery salvaged from that boat was snapped up on eBay, which meant that my original cash investment was not lost. My reputation at the boatyard is unfortunately in tatters, which is a shame because the actual owner of the yard and I got on very well, so much so that on several occasions I had really enjoyed providing musical entertainment for him on a pleasure cruise boat that he runs on the River Ouse.

Chapter 16

On leaving Denham Court in 1958 when I was fifteen; I was sent to live with foster parents, I found the new environment quite strange. I had been in the care system for five years, living in larger homes, with lots of other kids around me, following a completely different regime. Inside myself, I now felt like I was grown up enough to make my own decisions and find my own way, yet here I was living with another family who weren't my family; yet they were taking it upon themselves to tell me what I should be doing and when I should be doing it. That feeling of rebellion dogged me for quite a few years.

Looking for and finding my first job was an exciting time; starting a five-year apprenticeship to radio mechanics almost straight away. My piano lessons continued but with a different teacher, who didn't impart any valuable new musical knowledge to me the whole year that I was with her. She had me playing the same pieces of music and scale exercises every week, which were the required pieces for my exams; when all around me I would hear this new music, they called 'Rock and Roll'. Most of the older adults were decrying it as noise, while I couldn't wait to learn the words of the latest release on Radio Luxemburg or the BBC Light Program.

My dad would visit me occasionally; one day, even giving me his old bicycle, which meant I could join the cycle club at the factory, not that I was able to keep up on a ride out, with the more seasoned riders in the club.

I was encouraged to attend the Air Cadets, though I didn't manage to make any particular new friends; always seeming to be on the outside of social groups. I think trying to make friends and become socially accepted must be a universal problem.

My first foster parent, Nelly Ward was a frail elderly lady who had quite a challenging time of it, running a very small terraced house with her husband, young daughter, two grown up sons (who had both just finished their National Service) and myself to look after. She also worked a few hours down the week as a cook in a factory canteen. I am pretty sure that foster parents like her only took kids in for the money, not for the parenting. The Wards had given over their dining room to me for use as a bedroom. Every Sunday, that whole year I was with them, she prepared a roast beef dinner with blackberry and apple pie to follow. Every Sunday her husband, Jack, would make the same joke at the dinner table, intimating that we were having roast beef followed by blackberry and apple pie for a change this week. It was one of those households where all meals were taken in the small back parlour, the sitting room was only used on special occasions and young people should only speak when spoken to.

Other young people were wearing fashionable clothes; Nelly would have none of it. I was only allowed to wear what she had censored, which didn't help my social standing. In 1958 and the early sixties, young people followed quite a strict dress code, depending on what social group you were part of.

One time, when Nellie took me to the Co-op to buy a new jacket; owing to her poor eyesight, she didn't notice that the one I chose had silver specks in it that glinted when the light caught them. She was mortified when she saw me wearing it in the daylight and tried to take it back to the shop, but in those days, returning goods and complaining was quite often pointless, so I got to keep the jacket, She would take my wage packet of two pounds eight shillings off me each Friday and give me eight shillings back for my bus fares and spending money to last the week, so I helped the milkman with his deliveries on both Saturdays and Sundays when I could, for another five shillings. That is how my fifteenth year went, a whole lot better than Denham Court, though not as fancy free as I would have liked. It all changed when I became sixteen.

The Wards didn't want to take me with them on their summer holidays the next year, so my welfare officer had to temporarily move me to other foster parents for two weeks in July 1959.

Did I tell you about the welfare officer? Well, each of us in care had a welfare officer who was appointed by the council. It was their job to make sure that we were happy and that everything was alright. They were also partly responsible for writing in that care record I mentioned earlier. You only ever saw them in times of crisis, but you knew they were there if you should need them. My first welfare officer was a lady called Miss Henderson, she had a lot of empathy for my situation, and I liked her. However, I now had a new welfare officer, a man called Mr Bisham, he reminded me very much of Mr Hill at Denham Court; stern, with an attitude that said "I'm in charge"; I didn't get on with him. I couldn't understand why he would be in that job, when he made me feel like a stain on his shirt that he would sooner remove. He must have been well over six feet tall; in fact, he was a very large man and the funniest thing was to sit beside him in the new Austin Mini car he had just purchased and watch him drive across North London to the temporary foster parent's house. The car was obviously far too small for him as his knees were practically right up under his chin. That early model of the Mini has become a classic car now, you mostly only see them at classic car rallies they look tiny against modern cars.

Chapter 17

Jack and Louise Kible occupied the ground floor and basement of a three-storey house in New Southgate that had no front garden. You stepped out of the front door straight on to the pavement. In the next street were several families who had only recently emigrated from the West Indies. When the weather was nice, they would all be out on the street. The kids would be running about playing and the adults would have Calypso and Blue Beat music on so loud that even the houses would bounce. I had never seen people like this before. They were far more colourful in their dress than us. Even the men's trousers had an unusual cut, being sort of baggy in the middle. There was always a lot of happy noise and laughter down the street. This was so different from the quiet streets of net curtained windows around Finchley.

All of those lovely immigrants have long since been assimilated into our society. The houses we lived in at New Southgate have all been compulsorily purchased by the council, demolished and the area redeveloped. If you dare to start a party in the street like that now, you will probably have the police and the council on your back pretty quickly. Have we really made improvements to the way we live; or did we lose something along the way?

I was only supposed to stay with the Kibles for a fortnight while Nellie Ward and her family were on holiday. Jack and Louise had no children of their own and had never fostered before. They were so delighted at having a lad to look after; they couldn't do enough for me, even having me sleep in the bed between them a few times, which I found really embarrassing not knowing how I should behave. Louise would only be wearing a thin nightie; I would be able to feel the warmth and softness of her body against mine and Jack would encouragingly say,

"Go on son, give yur mum a cuddle".

I don't think they realised that I was sixteen. Both were pushing middle age; Jack had one eye that didn't appear to look in the same direction as the other. He was a very fit man, what they used to call 'a navvy'. He dug holes in the road for laying pipes and drains. The only power tool they had in those days was a pneumatic drill, there were no other mechanical diggers or power tools; it was all done by hand.

The upper two floors of the house were occupied by the Dales family who were in the Civil Defence and the St Johns Ambulance. They would often take me to St John Ambulance meetings with them, where I learnt basic first aid and bandaging.

Living with the Kibles was a whole new ball game, they had no silly rules, I found that I could come and go as I pleased, it was like being a grown up. Louise fed me with amazing meals; I mean spaghetti on toast with a fried egg on top, roast chicken on Sunday, jelly and tinned fruit flooded with cream.

I had my sixteenth birthday that July and spent the day at work bouncing about with a wonderful feeling of euphoria, telling my apprentice mates that I was legal now. That of course meant in relation to girls, especially Beryl; a bubbly petite teenage girl who was terrified of her dad finding out that she was hanging about with a boy.

It didn't take long for me to realise that life was better with the Kibles. I asked Jack and Louise if they would consider letting me stay with them. Unfortunately, my welfare officer had to arrange for any permanent transfer to them and he refused. I told you I didn't get on with him, never mind, Lady Luck stepped in again. The Dales who lived upstairs, had taken a shine to me and being members of the Civil Defence, they knew a lot of people who worked on the council. They must have had words with someone.

The day came when I was supposed to be taken back to the Wards, Jack said goodbye to me before he went to work, not expecting to see me again. Louise was in tears packing my case as I went off to work, but I somehow had an inner conviction that I would be staying with them. You can call it belief if you want; there was absolutely no reason for me to feel positive. Mrs Dale had told me that her efforts on my behalf had not born fruit and that Mr Bisham would be here at five-thirty when I got home from work, to take me back to Finchley and the Ward family, who were home from their holidays.

All day long at work that day I argued with myself.

"You're going back to the Ward's later. No, I'm not; I'll be allowed to stay with the Kibles."

"No such luck lad. Yes, there is, I'm staying".

My head was in turmoil until finally as I apprehensively pedalled my bike home from work and round the last corner to look down the hill that was the street where the Kibles lived, there was no little Mini car parked outside their house. Mr Bisham hadn't arrived. I had deliberately taken my time getting home, so I knew that if he wasn't there now, he probably never would be. As I entered the front door Louise jubilantly confirmed what I knew in my heart. I can't tell you how triumphant that felt. Almost like I had made a wish and it came true. The week of my sixteenth birthday and a place to live with foster parents who wanted me. That felt like another new start, a good positive one.

Nice to me as they were, things did turn a little bit sour when two Welsh lads turned up at the Kibles. They had quit their jobs in mining over in Wales and come to London looking for work; then having got a job working with Jack; he had offered them a bed; which turned out to be mine. This meant one of them sharing the bed with me and the other one sleeping on the floor of my room; although initially, for the first week, they had both insisted on squashing into the bed with me. I can tell you; it is not a pleasant experience having to share a bed with two whopping great sweaty men.

I usually, fell asleep listening to Radio Luxemburg on my little transistor radio, but these two guys even made me turn that off each night as they didn't like rock and roll.

#

Not much more than a year had passed since I left Denham Court and a little longer since I had seen Kenny Wolacott; in fact, I had completely forgotten about him having relegated him to the past. Then one Saturday afternoon while I was working in someone's back garden for extra money, there was the sound of a motorbike being ridden up and down the street, rather noisily for a quiet suburban neighbourhood. The engine stopped and about a minute later Kenny Wolacott came strutting down the garden path with a smile the size of an ocean on his face. He had an unusual way of bouncing as he walked; it was so distinct you could even recognise him from behind. Have you ever known anyone like that?

My mouth must have been hanging open in disbelief, because his grin soon turned to laughter. He never did let on how he knew where I was, he had ridden, what turned out to be a borrowed motorbike, all the way from Acton in West London specially to renew our acquaintance. The bike was a 500cc Matchless. As a learner rider there were no restrictions on the size of motorbike you could ride. Crash helmets were not compulsory until 1973, This was 1959. Kenny turned up in his shirt sleeves without a crash helmet. You could be seen as a bit of a sissy by other lads if you wore a 'Skid Lid'. Kenny was one who always had to prove his manhood; maybe because his father openly lived with another man in a gay relationship. Kenny's gran, whose house they lived in, took no notice of what was at the time, a criminal offence and later on; I met guys who were in prison for homosexual activity.

#

Life presents us with different desires as we move through it and from that day on, I had to have a motorbike. We apprentices attended the College of Further Education one day a week in Barnet; Not many weeks before Kenny turned up; one of the lads attending had been bought a Triumph 200cc Tiger Cub motor cycle for his sixteenth birthday. He was sitting astride it showing off in the college grounds with the engine ticking over. All of us lads were standing round drooling over it. I don't know what went through my mind, but I lifted my foot up and pushed the gear lever down, I think I was wondering what would happen? Anyway, the bike shot forward and he came off it causing some of the female onlookers to start giggling. Naturally, I wasn't too popular with his mates, not that I cared; I felt a thrill of satisfaction at his embarrassment, I'm pretty sure some of the other chaps felt the same.

It was never hard to find little back street cycle shops or shops that sold cheap motorbikes. The bike you bought probably wasn't going to be anything like new, in fact, it would probably be a bit of a wreck, but beggars can't be choosers and for a very small amount of money; £5 to be exact; I purchased an old Royal Enfield. It was so old that it had girder fork suspension on the back wheel instead of the more modern shock absorbers. In truth, if the engine ran, the brakes sort of worked, the lights came on and the tyres weren't quite bald, you were good to go. The biggest foe you had to be wary of was 'Old Bill' (the police) as the beat bobby wouldn't hesitate to pull you over. Then you would be given a ticking off at the roadside and because we didn't carry our documents about with us, the policeman would hand you a little notice giving you five days to produce your licence and insurance documents at the local Police Station.

Kenny Wolacott got himself an Ambassador two stroke motorbike. Like my Enfield, it was a bit past its best and made a horrendous noise. The racket they made was to their advantage as we took great pleasure in roaring down the high street on a Saturday morning, catching the attention of the weekend shoppers and having all the girls look admiringly round at us. Then we would go back for seconds just to see if any two girls were available for a chat up and pillion ride. You would be surprised at how often we pulled; (picked up a girl) if not in the high street then maybe at Alexander Palace fun fair, which was open all summer. Yes, there was no doubt; motorbikes held an attraction for us foolish youths.

Of course, you would want a better machine, especially when

you saw some of the beautiful motorbikes being ridden by guys down at the Ace Café on the North Circular Road. We only went a couple of times, owing to our bikes not comparing with some of those. I never wanted to be a fully paid up member to what were called 'The Ton-Up Boys' some of these riders used to have a 'Chicken Run'. The idea was to travel so many miles along the North Circular Road and get back to the Ace Café before the record on the jukebox had finished. The riders would ignore all traffic lights and disobey any speed control. Needless to say; there were quite a few accidents and untimely deaths.

I was quite content with my little machine; Kenny, on the other hand had other ideas. He threw his Ambassador motorbike over a bridge into the Grand Union Canal, and then told the insurance company that it had been stolen. I think they must have paid him out because he turned up one afternoon with a nice BSA 350cc motorbike. True; it was on HP (Hire purchase) but he must have found the deposit from somewhere and of course his gran, being a householder, signed as his Guarantor.

#

I have always felt that it was the Dales who informed Mr Bisham of the overcrowded conditions I was living in at the Kible's. The room I had to share with the Welsh guys was in fact the Kible's living room; they only had two other rooms, the kitchen diner and their bedroom. It wasn't just the Welsh guys sleeping in my room; Kenny often slept over because it was quite a ride back and forth to Acton, even in 1960 when there was a lot less traffic. Kenny's gran didn't like me staying at her house, not just because of the situation with his dad, but she thought I was a bad influence on him. Can you believe it? Anyway, the upshot is that Mr Bisham took it upon himself to move me to new foster parents. Pity, because I rather liked the freedom I was given by the Kibles despite the sharing and I hadn't been there more than about ten months.

So, here we go again, I gave a fond farewell to the Kibles and never saw Jack again. In later years, I used to see Louise sometimes, when I was out on business for the music shop. Now that the whole area where they used to live had been demolished and redeveloped into flats; it looked a lonely place and Louise looked like a lonely old lady every time I saw her. It made me really sad, though I never did stop to say hello.

Chapter 18

Mr Bisham had given me the name and address of the new foster parents who lived in Wood Green, not far from Tottenham Hotspur's football ground. He took my luggage in his Mini while I rode over on my motorbike. Charlie and Louise Hunt were waiting at the gate as my brakes almost didn't squeal me to a halt. Mr Bisham introduced us; Charlie Hunt was more interested in the motor bike I was riding than me. He went straight over to critically examine it. There was a shiny Vespa scooter parked on his drive so I straight away assumed that he was also a fellow who travelled on two wheels, which was correct, but I also quickly discovered that he did not think very much of my motorbike and by his tone it was obvious that he was unhappy for me to be riding it. I could see that his attitude had straight away ingratiated him with Mr Bisham. My thoughts went like this "I'm nearly seventeen I do not want to be fathered by this Welshman whom I don't even know." Of course, outwardly I smiled and agreed with him because twenty-one was when you reached independence in 1960, so I was still in the adult's 'Do as You're Told Land'.

Like the Kibles, the Hunts had no children, neither had they fostered before. I decided that I quite liked the way Charlie had taken on the role of dad and was over enthusiastic about my behaviour. I knew that he was trying to do the right thing by me.

Unlike the Kibles who didn't have any relatives living nearby; the Hunts had other family who lived around the corner as well as relatives not far away in Bounds Green. It was a nice feeling of being accepted when they took me to meet them all. The family around the corner had a grown-up son who used to race as a cyclist, but had given it up. His old racing bike was deteriorating in their garden shed. (That had a familiar ring to it;) however, they genuinely gave me the bike for nothing as I had offered to buy it and said that I would be happy to bring it back to life. It took a bit of work but was worth it. The other lads at the factory cycle club were quite envious of the handmade frame. Best of all was that on a ride out, I could just about keep up with them now. If you belong to a cycle club you will know that the pace can be pretty tough.

Charlie Hunt surpassed himself when I was knocked off that bike by a careless driver one Sunday afternoon while Kenny and I were on the cycle path coming back from a ride out to Southend. The driver of the car responsible was more involved with his lady passenger who was in a state of undress as he pulled across the cycle path in to the entrance of a small hotel. I should point out to you that the protective helmets worn by cyclist today were not around in the 1960's, we were happy to feel the wind in our hair as we rode. I felt lucky to have escaped serious injury; the bike however was un-rideable. Charlie borrowed an Austin 38 car and came to pick me and the wrecked bike up. He arranged for the bike to be repaired, which turned out to be a beautiful job, with new green paintwork and chrome fork ends; then one day, he went all the way to Cardiff, South Wales, on his Vespa scooter to see the chap who was responsible for the damage and get some compensation money from him. I gave Charlie full marks for effort. Not only that, but he decided to help me purchase a better motorbike by signing as an HP guarantor for a 125cc BSA Bantam which cost £22. We used my old motorbike as a deposit and I was to pay the balance monthly over two years.

#

My tenure with the Hughes only lasted six months before they tired of me. I was seventeen. I will tell you more later, but when they'd had enough of me, Charlie not only very wrongly took the BSA back to the shop, which was unfair as I had been making the payments regularly, but he also gave the racing bike back to his relatives around the corner. Which was even more unfair, as they had given it to me.

In a bewildered state; I was sent packing to a hostel in North Finchley, feeling like a discarded birthday present. So; I had lived with three different foster parents in just over two years.

#

The last straw for Mr Bisham was me wanting to leave my apprenticeship. At the time; I knew lads, including Kenny Wolacott, who were earning a great deal more than me, working on building sites as labourers. Mr Bisham made no secret of being fed up with me and demanded I give back all the tools and equipment that I had needed for the apprenticeship; which was another blow in the face for me as they could have been useful in another job. I can't imagine why he took them off me; I think it was just spite. Maybe he kept them for himself…. No, he didn't; he sold them to the firm I had been apprenticed with. Wasn't that nice of him?

The Hunts had been quite decent to me, even taking me to Guernsey with them for a two-week summer camping holiday. You might ask why our relationship went pear-shaped; well I think it was a combination of things. Firstly; there had been another one of those weird situations that had me completely embarrassed and confused; (like the Kibles action of having me in bed with them.) A couple of times, when only Louise and I were in the house, on coming out of my room, she would be naked in her bedroom with the door wide open, seemingly changing her clothes. She never looked embarrassed or made any attempt to hide herself. She just stood there and looked at me. Did she not realise that I was a mature lad now? I wouldn't like to make a judgement on that; I'll let you decide what was going on. Secondly; again, like the Kibles, they were a slightly older couple in their forties, who had no experience of raising children and the system had thrown them straight into looking after a troubled and rebellious teenager, it's no wonder they couldn't cope. But; unlike the Kibles who never seemed to worry about what I got up to; Charlie Hunt thought to make lots of rules for me to follow. They were probably perfectly sensible rules, had I been their own child, but the Hunts were, at that time, the eleventh guardians I'd had in my sixteen years of life. Some of whom were well meaning; some were not. All of these folks expected different things from me, they probably all had different motives for fostering or being carers. They certainly all had different standards and beliefs about how one should be. Why would I suddenly bend to a stranger's way of thinking? I'm afraid that notion also had me in conflict more than once.

The Hunts relatives in Bounds Green had a son; Keith, who was the same age as me. He was an apprentice baker. Keith had no friends as he worked long hours and was a bit of loner. Charlie and Louise made every effort to throw us together, obviously hoping that we would hit it off and we did, I really liked him.

When I first met him, Keith was a proper mummy's boy, he had no concept of getting up to mischievous things; at least, that is what the family thought of him; he was a 'Good Boy'.

It started with me going into the bakery at 4 am on a couple of Saturday mornings to help him make the bread dough. First, I rode over on the pushbike, but as it was a bit far, I started to use the motorbike. Then one afternoon I turned up at his house with Kenny and we were both on motorbikes. The effect on Keith of being with two tearaways like us was obvious; he just had to do something to prove he could be part of it and I have to tell you that underneath that sensible exterior he was a right nutter and a real daredevil. Imagine my surprise when he called for me at the Hunt's house, having persuaded his parents to let him buy a motorbike which was a Zündapp 175cc two stroke; quite a big bike, but Keith was a tall lad. The most amazing thing was the noise it made. I was out in the street cleaning the BSA Bantam and could hear a motorbike being heavily revved up somewhere in the distance above all the other suburban noise. I remember feeling a twinge of jealousy that someone had such a great sounding machine; then suddenly it was roaring down our road. I looked passed the parked cars to see a rider with his hair and his jacket flying in the wind, storming towards me with a massive trail of exhaust fumes following on behind. As I wasn't expecting it to be anyone that I knew, the machine was practically on top of me before I realised that it was Keith. He managed to stop, with some difficulty, not because the bike was unfit, no; it was the novice riding it who almost lost control. He sat there for a minute or so revving the engine, with a huge grin on his face completely oblivious to the disturbance he was causing on a normally quiet Sunday afternoon. An indignant Charlie Hunt came racing out of the house; with his slippers on and his bracers hanging down, newspaper in hand and his glasses falling off his nose, to protest at the noise. The expression on his face was a picture when he saw that it was his perfectly well-behaved nephew.

That's when the rot started setting in and before too long, I was being branded as a bad influence on Keith the lad who had this inner tiger just itching to be set free; only no one else seems to have seen it. I have no doubt, that is also what helped my downfall with the Hunts and Charlie's subsequent vindictive action of robbing me of everything I treasured.

Chapter 19

The Hostel in North Finchley that I was sent to, was not at all to my liking. I'd had my seventeenth birthday not long before and believed myself to be an adult with a craving for independence. Well, after two months I managed to persuade the authorities to let me move into my own digs. You have to remember that the council were under an obligation to look after my welfare till I was eighteen. Incidentally; the age of majority, that's when you can vote, was not lowered to eighteen from twenty-one until 1970. Anyway; I was asked for promises and assurances that I would behave responsibly. Kenny and I subsequently found a room in a house that was let out into separate bedsits. To us at the time; it was a palace that spelt 'Independence', but looking back, I would say that it was probably more than a bit tacky. The landlady lived on the ground floor, leaving all nine tenants to share one bathroom. I'm sure you can imagine that. We had two worn out arm chairs in our room that looked like they had been retrieved from the dump; they smelt like it as well. Two single beds, an old table and two chairs, a gas fire, a two-burner hob, a gas and an electric meter, a few cobwebs and a lot of damp wallpaper. The rent was £3 per week; we both had a job so it looked like we could pay our way; at least we would be independent. Mr Bisham didn't even bother to check that the room was suitable; I think he was hoping to wash his hands of me. That was early November 1960; I'm pretty sure that by the end of that month he did just that.

Chapter 20

I don't want you to think I've forgotten our modern world. Back here in the twenty-first century, we bought another boat. This cruiser arrived at the club when we owned *Ocean Magic*. I had seen and admired it with a secret wish to own her. Almost like witchcraft it came about. I have had the same thing happen to me with houses and life situations like moving to the Kibles. This is not always a conscious thing, it's something that you believe deep in your soul and then miraculously it happens. Possibly the power of positive thought; Have you learnt about that?

Moonbridge was a fibreglass boat, circa 1973; she came into our lives in 2014. She had teak decks and fly bridge. (That's a second steering wheel for enjoying pleasant weather outside the main cabin while cruising.) She was thirty feet long and slept four in two cabins. Outwardly she had very attractive lines and I put myself into the purchase of her whole heartedly, but once again; all that glitters is definitely not gold. Teak decks that leak and need re-caulking can cause huge damp problems in the cabins that are underneath them; as can leaky windows. The old saying applies here: 'caveat emptor' (buyer beware.) Unfortunately; my enthusiasm knew no bounds and landed me with a mountain of unexpected maintenance work, not the least of which was fixing a rather smelly sea toilet which had a leaky holding tank; nasty! I rose to the challenge as you can imagine, but eventually after nearly two years of fixing, mending and not much cruising, having used it more as a static caravan with the family for quite a few weekends; I decided it would be best if we parted company with her. So; *Moonbridge* went, leaving me free to chase my other dream of having a wide beam canal boat made as a shell and to fit her out myself from scratch. That way, any mistakes would be my own, not inherited ones from countless previous owners. You may be interested to know how that panned out later.

Chapter 21

Remember me telling you that my welfare officer let Kenny and I get a bedsit in 1960 with the idea that we would become independent? Well it didn't last long. Here we were; two seventeen-year-old tearaways hoping to make a go of it. No way!

Not long after our first day of independence we visited a working man's café for our lunch. That same evening, we went back to that café to help ourselves, as we were short of money. Of course, the café was closed, as we knew it would be. Kenny had noticed earlier that a window in the rear of the premises was not secured properly and would allow anyone access. Like taking sweets from a baby! We got in, took a couple of fruit pies and a tin of beans, nothing more and then made off. How stupid was that? Even more stupid was walking back to the bedsit along a main road, presuming that no one would see us carrying our ill-gotten gains at twelve o'clock at night.

Eee! Nothing like being inept. The streets, at that time would be deserted, not like now. Back then, everywhere closed and everyone went home to bed, so that by midnight it was like a ghost town. However, these two poor little fools who were carrying their loot home had not thought about 'Old Bill' patrolling the streets. He came on them just as they were crossing a railway bridge, so there was no escape. No jumping over a garden fence and legging it, in fact, no jumping over any fence, the bridge was too high. It went like this;

"Hello lads you're out late, what's in the bag?

And then;

"I think you had better get in the car and come down to the station".

Where we were charged with breaking and entering. The police noted us down as being of 'No fixed abode', which basically means, they won't let you out on bail, it seems there was some concern that we might abscond. As if!

In the morning, after we had spent a night in the police cells, the magistrate wouldn't deal with the case. He thought that stealing two fruit pies and a tin of beans was too serious for him, or maybe he thought, too stupid. We were remanded in custody for ten days pending reports. Remanded in custody means exactly what it says; in our case it was a prison cell each in Wormwood Scrubs prison; that is, after we'd had the pleasure of being taken there in a 'Meat Wagon'. Anyone suffering from claustrophobia probably won't survive that as it involved each prisoner being locked in a very small steel box on the coach, as well as being handcuffed.

Ten days is a very, very long time when you're seventeen and locked in a cell on your own for twenty-three hours a day. Well, time went by and after ten days; things still weren't resolved. That first ten-day remand ended up being six weeks. Six weeks in a nightmare. I was living in a cell, with only a tiny barred window that was too high to look out of, always listening for the sound of jangling keys outside the door that might signal the possibility of seeing another face, or maybe relief from boredom for a few minutes. Each morning, one of the other inmates would go from cell to cell, accompanied by a 'screw' (prison warder) with a trolley load of library books and old magazines. Meals were served downstairs but, you had to take them back to your cell to eat them. The only other times we were let out of the cells was first thing in the morning to get a jug of water for washing and to empty the potty that you had to use for weeing and pooing; they called it 'Slopping Out'. Then, later there were two half hour periods of exercise; one in the morning and one in the afternoon, which involved walking round the prison yard in a big circle. We were sent to 'The Scrubs' at the beginning of November; eventually, six weeks later, just before Christmas, we finally appeared at the Middlesex Quarter Sessions to answer the charge and both Kenny and I received a three-year probation sentence.

I am not forgetting about my transgression when I remind you that I was supposed to be under the care and protection of the Middlesex County Council till age eighteen. At no time did they come to my aid. I'm not suggesting that one could behave as one liked and get away with it, but where, might you ask, was my welfare officer, Mr Bisham while all this was going on? You've got a young lad who has committed a very minor offence locked up in an adult prison. Did Mr Bisham come to my aid? Speak up for me? Arrange for me to get bail, have me supervised in a hostel? Help in any way? Nope! Mr Bisham was conveniently poorly and unavailable the whole six weeks. He even sent a junior assistant to speak for me in court at the last minute. This assistant knew nothing about me and completely mixed my history up with Kenny Wolacott's when speaking to the court. I told you Mr Bisham wanted to wash his hands of me and it seems that he did. I have, since, held the council to account for the sexual abuse that I suffered while in their care. What a pity I can't hold them to account for their lack of compassion and understanding of a troubled youngster's needs.

#

Now, I want you to imagine that you are seventeen years old and you have been locked away from the world for six weeks in a cell measuring about 7ft x 10ft. Close your eyes think about it. You may feel that you will be elated to be free and it's true, you will, but what you may not think of is the fear, when suddenly confronted by a noisy world, with all the hub-bub, where everything is rushing around you. Something you normally take for granted, like crossing a busy road, has become a very challenging experience; you feel like an alien who has just landed on earth. Yes, I'll grant you that after an hour or so you will probably be more or less back to the normal street wise person you were before you were shut away. In the meantime, let us hope you keep your nerve and stay safe. It's just another aspect of care that no one seemed to be aware of.

Chapter 22

On leaving court, I was handed a travel warrant and told to make my way to a hostel in Southall. Kenny trundled off back to his grandma's with his dad who had spoken up for him in court. The manager of the hostel hadn't wanted to accept me and made it clear that he would have his eye on me. Great start! To make matters worse, I was wearing the only clothes that I owned and that included the leather jacket from my lost motorbike days. It wasn't a cheap one; I'd saved up and bought it out of my meagre apprentice wage. I thought it looked pretty smart, real leather with a fur lining. That jacket certainly helped me pull a few girls. Anyway; he hated it and made no effort to hide his displeasure. No leather jackets and no Skin tight jeans! If I'd had another jacket, I swear he would have taken it off me right there. As it happens, he stole it from the cloakroom a few weeks later when I was at work; then he tried to make out that one of the other lads had taken it. I quizzed all nine of them, then I saw it hanging in his office a few days later, it wasn't true, he took it alright and that just left me with my work donkey jacket to wear. Still, it would amuse me to buck the system, by locking myself in the toilet one Saturday afternoon, with needle and thread, to sow the legs of my jeans up so that they were tighter and looked more fashionable. (Sewing lessons given by Bertha Helped).

#

What is it about kids in care that seems to attract an unhealthy number of weirdos? I know what you're thinking, "They've put controls in place to stop that sort of thing now". Let's hope so!

There was this guy, Mr White he called himself; would arrive at the hostel on a Saturday afternoon to take one of the boys out in his car. He would only ever take out one boy at a time. We were all sixteen- and seventeen-year-olds. The other lads seemed to know about him and one or two of them would express a desire, when talking amongst ourselves, to go on an outing with him as apparently, he would let you have a drive of his Austin Cambridge car. I watched a boy get out of Mr White's car one day and asked him if Mr White had let him drive, He sheepishly admitted that "Yes, he did".

Well, as you now know, I have had some experience of abuse and abusers and I knew that this guy was one. This is the problem. How to get what you want from a man like that and keep the situation under control? What I wanted, was to drive the Austin Cambridge; I made up my mind that Mr White would be the one taken for a ride, not me!

Having put myself forward as a well-behaved boy and one who really needed a treat, the hostel manager actually consented to me going out with Mr White one Saturday afternoon saying

"You've shown me that you can toe the line lad, blah! de blah!"

Off I went with the weirdo. When we got about two miles down the road, I wondered out loud to him, if he would trust me to have a drive of his car.

"Do you know how?" was his question

What a silly question; I've never driven, but I've watched; how hard can it be?

"I've driven loads of cars" was my confident but dishonest reply.

So, he pulled over on a quiet stretch of road, eager; as I knew he would be, to get me at what he thought was a disadvantage; we swapped seats; a bench seat in those cars by the way and brrm! brrm! I was driving. A bit all over the road at first but I soon got the hang of it. Besides; I knew not to stop, as that would put me at a disadvantage.

Mr White; well, he was allowed to put his hand on my left leg in the pretence of helping me to operate the clutch pedal, as he fondled his stiffy through his smart trousers with his other hand. I went out with him a few times and gained valuable driving experience, in fact, they were the only driving lessons I ever had (If you can call it that) while Mr White had to content himself with a right hand on my left leg and a left hand for personal comfort! Tough world isn't it?

You can't accuse me of having no work experience at seventeen. My apprenticeship had me doing all kinds of jobs from wiring looms and soldering to casting metals and making tools in the old style, by hand. While there, I moonlighted doing part time work helping a milkman. After terminating the apprenticeship I worked on a building site, in a timber yard, in Woolworths as a store keeper (but I got sacked for tardiness after two weeks) plus a bakery where I only lasted one morning as I found feeding pies into an oven for four hours about as interesting as watching paint dry. In the sixties, you could walk in and out of jobs like changing your underwear. You would go to the Labour Exchange (which is now the Job Centre) and walk out again with a card in your hand to take to an interview introducing you to another potential employer; who would look you over, ask if you had your P45 and National Insurance card, and tell you to start at eight o'clock in the morning, or whatever time they started.

The second job I got while at the hostel was at a tyre fitting depot. The boss was called Len West. You could tell that he was a businessman as he drove a flashy Vauxhall Cresta and always wore a suit. He would be out on business most of the time, leaving me to run the depot. I liked that, not so much the job as being trusted and given some responsibility. The equipment that is used in tyre garages today wasn't around in 1961; everything was done with hand tools like tyre levers and big hammers, so it was hard work, but it didn't matter to me as it gave me a chance to show off my muscles and how clever I could be.

I had to travel on busses back and forth from Southall to the garage in Hayes, so at the beginning of April Mr West suggested that perhaps I could move into digs just around the corner with a lady he knew who took in lodgers. I put it to the hostel manager, he checked with the council, they agreed, so, after three months in the hostel I was off on my own again. Mr West further thought that I should have my own mode of transport and provided me with a Lambretta scooter, saying that I could pay him back weekly out of my wages.

Displaying a tax disc on your vehicle is only a distant memory now as in the computer age; the DVLC has found no need for them. In 1961 the police would take great pride in stopping a young motor cyclist to check that he was displaying one. My Machiavellian mind led me to removing a tax disc off an accident wrecked motorbike and putting it on my own scooter thinking to get out of paying road tax. Surely 'Old Bill' would only scrutinise the date on the disc which was in big letters. However, when a police man did survey my scooter, he looked closely at the disc and noticed that the registration number on it did not match the registration number on my bike. Oh dear! I was given three months detention as I had broken my probation. That was the downside. The upside was that my three years' probation were cancelled and with remission for good behaviour I only served two months detention.

The government closed borstals and detention centres in 1982 as there was a lot of abuse found to be going on. In detention you had no privileges, only heavy physical exercise and work as it was supposed to be a 'Short Sharp Shock'. No, don't feel sorry for me, I had a great time. I bet you're imagining these poor youths dragging their ball and chain around a prison yard. Well it wasn't like that. A lot of shouting and threatening behaviour from the 'screws' but apart from being hauled out of bed at 5.30 am each morning and doing physical jerks out on the square before breakfast, rain or shine, it was fun. Actually, it was a great summer and I left there in July looking super fit and brown as a berry. The fact is that you just had to think positive to survive.

#

The family Mr West had recommended I lodge with were Irish and lived in a council house on an estate. They reminded me of Jack and Louise Kible in one sense; very rough and ready. But unlike the Kibles; this couple had a sixteen-year-old daughter. If my welfare officer had checked their house, he probably wouldn't have let me move in there. Reading the notes made on my care record at the time though, clearly shows that with my eighteenth birthday only months away, the council were happy to shed the responsibility. I myself had got to the point where I was happy not to be reliant on them.

Chapter 23

Both Mr West and my new landlady promised to keep a place for me when I went off to serve detention. The landlady; Mrs McIntyre, even came to visit me at the detention centre. She fetched me some cigarettes and matches which I couldn't have because smoking was a privilege that wasn't allowed. Prisoners were searched after visits so I asked her to hide them in the toilets for me and then collected them later when I was cleaning the administration block where the toilets were. I've told you that to give you an insight into how close my relationship had become with these people. At least; so I thought!

On leaving detention in July, I returned to the digs and the tyre fitting job in Hayes. That same week I had my eighteenth birthday and received an uncompromising letter from the council absolving themselves from all future responsibility for me. They didn't waste any time, not even to ascertain that I was set up alright. Mr West had made a pretence of keeping my job open for me, but had taken on another lad while I was away, so at the end of my first week back, he gave me the sack. The laws controlling things like unfair dismissal were not in place in 1961. You got the sack and that was that; no job.

Things haven't changed much for lodgers either; you can still be kicked out if the householder wants to be rid of you. I suffered that as well about two weeks later. It seems the McIntyre family had a middle-aged Irish truck driver called Murphy lodging with them when I returned; he was a large ginger haired guy in his thirties who had a tipper truck parked outside and snored like a pig when he was asleep. Theirs was a small three bedroomed terraced council house. Guess where the Irishman was sleeping. That's right; I had to share a bed with him. With nowhere else to go I had no choice. The thing is that I caught him one night sharing their daughter's bed. The McIntyres had no clue, not even that he was the one who got her pregnant. This fornication must have been going on for quite a while as the pregnancy was only discovered because the daughter, who was a very round girl anyway, was starting to look even rounder. Murphy did a disappearing act with his truck, the daughter wouldn't tell her parents that he was the man who had been screwing her and I had arrived back after two months, just in time for them to assume that it was me who got her pregnant before I went away. I can tell you in no uncertain terms that I 'wouldn't have touched her with a barge pole'. I have no idea how it all turned out, as I was unable to pack my bag fast enough and leg it out of the front door. Her dad, who was also a very large Irishman, chased me down the road waving a hammer in the air shouting unmentionable abuse after me and adding that he would swing for me if he ever saw me again.

I managed to get a room in a lodging house around the corner; where the landlady's husband Mr Carter, had just taken me on to work in his decorating business. I was apprehensive about being so near to the McIntyres, even though I knew that I could handle myself if need be, having only recently been forced into a fight with a bully boy while in detention. That little fisticuff had cost me two days in 'chokey' (locked in a cell with only bread and water) while my adversary had nursed quite a few more bruises than me in his cell next door. However, my fears about the Mad Irishman were allayed by the new landlady's son Joe, who had just finished serving his National Service in the army and must have thought himself a hard case, because he made it clear that he would sort the Irishman out if he gave me any trouble. He sounded so convincing that I felt between the two of us we could probably win a war. National Service, which was compulsory for all males on reaching the age of eighteen, was abolished in December 1960.

Have you ever noticed how much useful junk people dump in sheds and garages? Well, the Carters had a lean to garage at the bottom of their garden where they would park a Ford Pilot V8 engine car; which was interesting in itself, but against the back wall was a 350cc Enfield Bullet motorbike that was Joe's and had been sat there unused for two years while he did his National Service. Joe preferred to drive the V8 Pilot now, saying that he had outgrown the bike. Just what I needed! After some cleaning and tinkering the bike roared into life, Joey had a quick go on it, but wasn't too keen anymore, I think he thought to pull more 'crumpet' (Girls) with the V8. He handed the Enfield over to me, not to own, just to use whenever I wanted, so I used it, a lot!

First chance I got I gunned that Enfield down the Western Avenue past Park Royal to Acton, turning up at Kenny Wolacott's gran's house where I knew he was living; my turn to surprise him. It's ok; we stayed out of trouble as a duo, but he was already in trouble, just that the shit hadn't hit the fan yet. Still on probation, he had a fourteen-year-old girlfriend who was showing early signs of being pregnant. We spent a few weeks having fun at the weekends then at the end of November the bubble burst for me. Mr Carter said he didn't need me any more so I lost my job and was also asked to find new lodgings, just like that and of course, no more motorbike. No reasons or excuses, my room was needed for someone else. How come so many people like to give with the right hand and then take away with the left? Ce la vie.

#

So here I am; Just eighteen years old, no job, nowhere to live and very little cash. I decided to head down to Acton, at least I had a mate there; maybe his gran would take pity on me. No such luck, she actually had the nerve to tell me that I was a bad influence on her grandson; little did she know what was coming. I did manage to sneak round to the back door and join Kenny in her kitchen several times when she was out or gone to bed, we would share a tin of tomato soup or a sandwich. I also huddled down behind her garden shed more than once to shiver my way through the night with just an overcoat Kenny stole from his dad for me to use as a blanket. After a week I hadn't managed to find a job, the weather was turning more wintery and I had no cash to pay for a room which would usually be one week in advance.

One very cold evening, when I was aimlessly wandering around the streets looking for some shelter for the night; a man who called himself 'Mr Jones' pulled up in his car and offered to give me a bed for the night. I accepted in desperation, but it turned out to be a bed for certain sexual services. Being a lad of some experience in these matters, I was able to keep him on a promise and then sneak away with some money from his wallet when he went to sleep.

Sunday morning found me bunking a tube train bound for Petticoat Lane with the intention of stealing food from the stalls under cover of the crowds of people that used to visit the Sunday market there.

It wasn't child's play like I thought it would be; an apple did find its way into my pocket, but then when a careless punter dropped some loose change, I took the opportunity to pick some up and run as fast and as hard as I could. Some people gave chase; I don't know how many because I didn't look back. I could hear their shouts behind me "Stop him" and "Stop thief" and I knew that folk in front of me were turning around to see what the commotion was, so I started pointing up ahead of me and shouting as I ran "Stop thief."

That confused the on lookers enough to let me get away. At the end of the lane I jumped on to the passenger platform of a moving double decker bus leaving them all behind. That may have sounded like a daring feet of desperado to you, but I can tell you; when I sat down on that bus and the adrenaline had subsided, I was absolutely shaking with fear from the stupidity of what I had just done. In my imagination I saw myself being beaten up and lynched by an angry mob. Still, when I got my composure back, a couple of shillings proved to be very useful.

The last straw for me was going to the National Assistance board to ask for help. They call it the Social Security nowadays; it was never easy to negotiate. The officer on duty gave me a bus pass to travel across London to Peckham where there would be some food and a bed for the night in some kind of hostel. I suppose you could call it a bed; actually, it was a mattress on the floor. The queue outside the building must have been about fifty strong. Although that's a bad choice of words, as the strongest thing was the smell. Every single body in that queue was an elderly neglected man; save one lady that I noticed jostling with all the men. Some had whiskers so long that you could stand on them; many had clothes in rags, unwashed bodies, feet that shuffled along the pavement in hopelessness, they were the very people that Ralph McTell sang about later in his song 'The Streets of London'.

Today, we see unfortunate people of all ages sleeping on pavements; some even pitch a tent in a doorway. In 1961, the police would move loafers and loiterers along; there was no sleeping in doorways. I felt so ashamed to be there; I didn't see any other young people. I made a resolve to make the most of that mattress with a blanket on the floor, the squashing together on those mattresses, the dishwater soup and dry bread supper, the coughing and retching and the stink of unwashed bodies. In the morning I would get up and bunk a ride on the tube train (ride without paying) back to my comfort zone in Acton to sort this out.

The 'dosshouse' had come as a wakeup call, it's amazing what you can do with your senses and resolve. I was back at the labour exchange in Acton by 8.30 am with renewed determination. Then, having an interview for a job on the railways by 10.30 am where I was asked to start work the next day which was Tuesday. I still didn't have a room; neither did I have any cash to rent one.

Kenny came up with a couple of shillings from somewhere; probably his gran's purse, for me to buy food. I roughed it in a shed at the railway yard for two nights. When the foreman found out about my situation, he very kindly advanced me a sub on my wages and sent me to see a lady with a bedsit to rent down the road. I wouldn't be sleeping rough or visiting a 'dosshouse' again thanks to that man's kind thoughtfulness.

Christmas 1961 came and went, Kenny's younger brother 'Ginger' joined the army in January; Kenny came and told me about it. We were both disgusted. We had vowed never to do anything so stupid; we valued our freedom too much.

In March Kenny triumphantly proclaimed to me that he also had joined the army. Do you remember that business of him and probation and getting a fourteen-year-old girl into trouble? Well he was under the mistaken impression that if he was in the British army, he could get away with it. I have to say that information was not as freely available before the internet and much shared knowledge was just hearsay. Kenny was more than likely hoping that values from a hundred years before were still valid. Anyway; having no other close friends, I went the next day to sign up for six years in the army myself. Looking back; I realise that I hadn't considered the prospect of a career and a home in the army; I had just bungled into it following a friend who was, in a way, the only family that I had available to lean on. There is a lesson in life here: You are your own person, stand tall and don't rely on others. Just two weeks into our 'Basic Training' the authorities did of course turn up and haul Kenny off on various charges which had him kicked out of the army and landed in Borstal for two years.

Chapter 24

In the Royal Dragoons, I found the discipline easy to handle and was posted to Germany for training on tanks attached to the 16/5th Lancers. On arriving back to the UK in 1963, I joined the Royals who were an armoured car regiment but now had to convert to tanks. By the time summer vacation came I was bored with the army regime which consisted of cleaning tanks, having them inspected, then taking them out on Salisbury Plains to make them dirty again as we played soldiers. Pointless parades on the barrack square and just when you had a date with a girl in the town you were put on guard duty where you walked around the barracks at night with a pickaxe handle for a weapon in case of trouble. Playing soldiers seemed like a waste of time to me. I'd learnt to drive a tank, operate a radio, fire a gun, how to polish brasses and shine a pair of boots. All of this was stuff you were told to do, leaving very little room for the use of personal initiative. The crowning glory was a new troop officer, who arrived straight out of junior officer training school; was younger than me and clearly didn't merit my respect as I knew more about life, tanks, shining boots and our weaponry than he did, which I know, is not the right thought process for a soldier. Lol.

The only way to prematurely leave the army was to buy oneself out, but I had no money so AWOL. (absent without leave) was the only option. I went to Edinburgh to stay with an army pal, Johnny Alex, in August for our summer break; he was as disenchanted with army life as me, we both decided not to go back to camp. In order to avoid detection, we changed our names, making ourselves into two brothers. No need to steal someone else's identity as we even doctored our birth certificates with ink remover, a pen and some clever forgery while on the train from Edinburgh to London. The trains were still steam driven then and used to take several hours for that journey. Once in London we obtained new National Insurance work documents by telling the officials that we were gypsies and had no papers or records. I wonder if one could still do that in our world of illegal immigrants and computers.

I had a couple of quiet months leading up to Christmas 1963 being responsible, working with a decorating firm, paying my way and managing to buy an Ariel Leader motorbike for travelling to work.

I was riding the Ariel to work when I first saw Frances; she was walking to work herself. It was a crisp November morning; the cold air had made her nose red and it matched her bright red hair. When I got to meet her, I learnt that she had dyed her hair red, but hadn't expected such a strong colour. It obviously embarrassed her, so she tried to tone it down with bleach and then ended up with bright pink hair instead. How many of you girls have had a similar disaster?

Sometimes I would take Frances to the pub, where we would listen to the live bands playing. A well-known band had once appeared in the village hall not far from the army camp in Tidworth where I was stationed. I was in awe of anyone standing on stage, entertaining like that, but unfortunately the squaddies didn't appreciate the singer, whose stage wear was a fancy pink suit; then with all the shouting and booing the band finally left the stage, only to be replaced by a chap with a record player, which wasn't quite the same experience. At twenty years of age, I never would have imagined that one day I myself would earn a living as a singer and musician.

Johnny Alex and I had split up as he preferred to go 'Up West' (to London) to make his fortune, but he didn't fare too well having been taking drugs. When he heard that my decorating job had finished, he asked if I would move to Notting Hill to share a bedsit with him. I was in a relationship with Frances and later we got married, but at the time, a full-on relationship wasn't what I wanted, so I moved to Notting Hill in January 1964. Having no job meant that once again I was going to have to rely on my wits.

Chapter 25

Have you ever had that feeling of elation when you achieve one of your aims or long term goals; maybe something that you've dreamt about doing, tried to work towards, or an item you set your heart on having; always believing you can get there, maybe occasionally doubting yourself as time drags on, but always coming back to your faith? You visualise yourself in that position, owning, or going to, or doing what might, at times, seem impossible. I hope that you can feel the seeds of that optimism throughout this book as I don't want it to be a negative discourse. I think it was Marcus Aurelius who said "Our doubts are our traitors" More than 2000 years ago. Believe in yourself.

Is that how I found myself watching a mobile crane lowering a forty foot by ten-foot-wide beam shell into the River Ure at Newby Wharf on a cold December morning in 2016? The boat builders had taken exactly six weeks to weld it into shape and spray the inside with insulation foam, now they were launching and testing it for me. That done, I was invited to step aboard and take her away, with handshakes and nods of approval all round, off I went, heading for my mooring at the boat club. There may have been a winter wind blowing that day, with the threat of rain in the air, but with my waterproof coat pulled tight and the hood up over my head as I grasped the boat tiller, all I could sense was that feeling of elation I mentioned a while ago. Looking at the scene on this impressive stretch of river (where the army engineers used to practice laying bridges over rivers and where the Nidd Ferry sunk in 1869 with the loss of six lives), put me in mind of that thing people say about how one might be forgiven for thinking they had died and gone to heaven, even on this winter's day, you could feel a peaceful tranquillity in the air while cruising this wide stretch of river at four knots.

The boat hull was moored up on my mooring at the club and there it sat, empty. Luckily, I had drawn out a plan on graph paper to let the boat builders know exactly where to fit the windows and to help me with the interior layout. The idea was to produce a boat that you can live aboard or cruise. Having an empty boat shell was quite a challenge. 'A blank canvas', it meant researching what could and what couldn't be done with things like the electric circuits and gas pipes, how to fix up a solar power system that's viable, or how many batteries will be needed so there are enough amp hours of power available when you need it? You have to carefully plan cable runs and fuse box connections, wiring for lights and plugs, pipes for plumbing the galley and bathroom, pumps for water and waste plus where to put fixings for walling partitions and the ceiling. Then there is the boat safety test to consider, which is a bit like the MOT needed on your car. The 'BSC' didn't exist in 1976 when I bought my first boat. Various boating disasters like gas systems blowing up, have led the authorities to introduce it. I have always been a hands-on sort of guy, what you might call a doer, so the challenge was on.

With the availability of the internet our modern world is so good at providing information; anything you want to learn about, or buy is there for the asking. Before the internet we would go to the library searching for a book or two that covered the subject we were interested in. The supply chains for tools and materials are endless now, not like when I was young, where a small DIY shop on the corner was the best you would get and skills were mostly handed down from one person to another in a more personal manner; you can learn those skills on your computer now. The fit out took me eighteen months, working at it for a few hours almost every day. The Mazda van I was driving at the time proved invaluable for hauling all the heavy parts, timber and equipment to the boat. Once again I found myself so pleased to be a musician, living a life my father would have called 'pie in the sky' so grateful for those early piano lessons while in care that have given me the chance to pass on some music knowledge by teaching others and still having time to spare for chasing rainbows. Mind you, my rainbows haven't always been boats; a fresh shower on a sunny day will always produce a new rainbow; like life without a mortgage or rent for instance, now there's a pretty big one.

#

On getting divorced from my first wife Frances in 1981, I was left with a mortgage and two teenage children (Paula and Trevor) to look after. Nothing unusual about that you might say and you would be right, I'm sure thousands of folks live that way. After my upbringing, there was no way I would abandon my kids. A way forward from that state is one of those rainbows you chase. Finish doing up the house, sell it, make a small profit and buy another house, hopefully with a smaller mortgage next time. Sound good to you? That's great if you are able and have the time to spare for all the work or maybe the finances to pay someone else to do it.

Having taken eighteen months to renovate and decorate the whole house I began to avidly study the property ads in the local papers. One Friday I noticed the council were asking for cash offers on a detached Georgian property in Knaresborough that they were threatening to place a closing order on. That's them saying the property was unfit for human habitation and needed to be upgraded or pulled down. Trevor and I went to look at it. Oh dear! What a mess, it had obviously been empty and neglected for many years. Not one of the Georgian panes of glass had been left unbroken, doors had been smashed in and there was a lot of wood rot, but heh! It had what looked like a solid roof, now that can't be bad... can it? My cash offer was in the post that night. Our house had already been valued, so I was able to work out how much cash might be available if we found a buyer for it. Considering the potential, the property in Knaresborough had, my offer was tiny, but it was all I would be able to afford without borrowing. I was pretty sure some developer or someone with

101

more cash would make a better offer and be accepted, but I knew that a large part of me was still looking with optimism at going over that rainbow. About a month later, my surprise and delight on receiving a letter from the council accepting the offer I'd made, was no less diminished by me believing it could happen. That'll be me mortgage free if I can pull it off!

If you want to carry out your own conveyancing and save hundreds of pounds in solicitor's fees there is a book to explain how to do it; also of course, nowadays, information and knowledge online. In 1981, I bought the book. The biggest problem I came up against was the resentment of a real solicitor working for the vendor I was purchasing from. It's not rocket science transferring ownership of a house it's just filling in a few forms, paying a couple of small fees and waiting for the replies with fingers crossed that there will be no complications. The vendor's solicitor, who wasn't very cooperative or amenable from the start, accidentally on purpose, I think, lost one of the forms that I'd sent him. Luckily for me, I had registered the posting so his little bit of (what I suspected) to be sabotage, only served to delay matters, which would have peeved all the other parties involved or even made the deal fall apart. Childish! You can't stop enterprise.

It was late November when Trevor and I moved into the house in Knaresborough that the council would have knocked down and redeveloped. We made one tiny room; which could just about hold all of our boxed possessions, habitable. Cooking was going to be on a small camping stove and then we had a bucket for everything else. The biggest surprise we found on moving in were the other inhabitants; mostly mice and butterflies. There having been no windows in the house for many years, all kinds of wildlife had taken up refuge there. The mice would pop out as we sat eating or watching television. Sitting with a loaded airgun proved to be a useful and amusing pastime. The butterflies just kept hatching out as we made the house more secure and consequently warmer, which was a great shame for them because it was winter outside and they probably wouldn't have survived.

Trevor's sister; Paula; who had just turned eighteen, chose not to move in with us, but instead found lodgings with a friend who lived nearer to her job in Leeds.

To me, it didn't matter that there was no money left in the bank for renovations, as I was being paid well singing in a band that had once been at the top of the pop charts and to think, when I was discharged from the army, that naïve officer I told you about, had put a comment in my service discharge book, 'Would probably be able to do a useful job of unskilled work in civilian life.' What a twat! I wonder if he knew the importance of believing in yourself.

Chapter 26

Now here's a thing; in 1964 I ended up sharing a bedsit in Notting Hill, the whole world before me and three 'Queenies' living downstairs. These were transvestites, who would dress up in drag of an evening complete with wigs, looking more like eighteenth century tarts than modern day women; then they would patrol the Bayswater Road W1 opportuning any willing males driving by. In the short time that I knew them, they were beaten up more than once by disappointed males who thought they were pulling a female and arrested by the police more than once as well. They were always upbeat about their situation even though every aspect of what they did was liable to get them worked over or put in prison. One of these gentile chaps fancied me and would lend me his driving licence.

It hadn't been difficult for Johnny and me to start a decorating business, we were even lucky enough for a client in Kensington Square to let us borrow her minivan, which is why the loaned licence was very useful.

Things were working out pretty well living in Notting Hill and then one day Frances, who was sixteen at the time, came over from Southgate on the tube train, wanting to let me know that she was pregnant. That put a spanner in the works for us both, but at the time, we didn't know what we should do about it. Frances was quite accepting of her situation, I knew that I was responsible, but had no clue how we should move forward. I was absent from the army, using a wrong name, sharing a tatty bedsit in Notting Hill and struggling to start a decorating business. Then in March Kenny was released from Borstal. Once again, he managed to locate my whereabouts and turned up like a bad penny, at the bedsit. I was glad to see him because Johnny had been disappearing for days on end; then showing up again stoned out of his head; he eventually disappeared from my life completely and I never knew what became of him. With Kenny; the extra hands would be useful in the business. Well, one thing led to another and one day Kenny expressed a desire to go to visit his younger brother Ginger who was still in the army, having recently married and was renting a cottage in Hampshire. Good idea! Let's borrow Ernie's licence and the minivan, then drive down to Hampshire to surprise him.

Not such a good idea. On arriving at the cottage, Ginger's wife was horrified to see his errant brother and I on her doorstep. Polite hello's, a cup of tea and don't hurry back here as you may corrupt my husband, were the order of the day. I think the visit lasted about thirty minutes! (That was only beaten by a 350-mile drive to Cornwall in later years with Danni to see my mother, a visit which lasted about ten minutes!) While driving back to London from Hampshire we were stopped by the police in the early hours on a quiet country road. How ironic was that; drive around in London with no licence and no insurance with all the traffic, if you behaved yourself you would be fine (not today, of course, with all the cameras), but be seen on a quiet country road, two likely looking lads driving a minivan registered to an address in Kensington, London. Boom! boom! You're nicked. Guess what? Fingerprints taken at the police station and they knew who we really were, one fresh out of Borstal and one absent from the army. Put them in a cell in case they do a bunk! My God! Not again.

The police released us after keeping us on remand for a week while doing their inquiries. Ernie had originally told them that I stole his licence, but then he decided to come clean when the police pressured him about being a 'homosexual'. No freedom for me though, as the MP's were waiting to haul me back to the army camp and yet another cell, only this time, it was in the guardhouse at the army camp. In a way, I was glad to be facing the music with the possibility of getting kicked out of the army, although that was by no means certain. Frances and I were still in touch with each other and I was beginning to see that if I could get out of this army situation, we could make a fresh start together. On the other hand; I'd been hauled away from what might have been a promising business in Notting Hill, having recently quoted for some lucrative subcontract work decorating ten newly converted single bed apartments and won the contract.

There was another lad waiting for a court martial with me while I was in the guardhouse, we had to wait a month before the army convened it. We were both locked in a cell at night, but during the day, the cell doors were left open and we were given various jobs to do. One of my jobs was cleaning the RSM's (Regimental Sergeant Major's) office which had a notice board on the wall with a roll of all the personnel in the regiment. There were two separate smaller lists on the board; one was headed 'Should be corporal', and had six names on it, the other was headed 'Should be sergeant' this had four names on it. To my complete astonishment, my name was on both lists. Do you know; if I'd been told that I had prospects I would never have gone AWOL. Oh well, too late now, the die was cast.

The month went by pretty quickly; it was helped by me hitting it off with the other guy who had always been the camp comedian, we called him Mousey. We also had a little adventure going on where I was able to open and close my cell door at night with a piece of wire. I would get out of my cell when the guard were all quiet, let Mousey out of his cell, then we would slip out into the back yard, climb through the barbed wire on top of the wall and disappear to the Naffi Club for a chat and hopefully someone buying us a beer. (We didn't have any money.) It was a little more awkward to climb back in to the yard but with practice, we got better at it.

The sergeant of the guard came into the Naffi one evening, while doing his rounds, he did a double take at Mousey and I sat with some other lads. He must have thought he recognised us, but said to himself, "No, it couldn't be, I only locked them up an hour ago".

As soon as he'd gone, Mousey and I hightailed it back to our cells. We only just managed to get back about two minutes before he came in to check on us. Phew! I wonder what he was thinking?

One hundred and twelve days was the sentence handed out by the court martial without any mention of my services not being required any more. That meant being sent to Colchester army prison, to serve their version of a 'Short Sharp Shock', hard labour and retraining. For me, it was another one of those belief moments; in my head I couldn't conceive of being kept in the army, I just didn't believe it was my fate, even when we were loaded onto a truck and transported to Colchester.

There inside the gates of Colchester forces prison, waiting for the order to dismount from the truck, I could see various squads of prisoners around the square, being shouted at and made to run (double) everywhere, but still something in my head was saying "This isn't right." A loud, aggressive sergeant came around to the back of the truck with a clipboard, he started barking orders for all those 'misfits' whose names he called out to dismount with their kit and get in line. When he had finished, both Mousey and I were the only ones left on the truck, all the other prisoners had dismounted and were standing in line with their kitbags, looking like a new set of victims for the sergeant. There was a lot of puzzlement and discussion amongst the sergeant and other NCOs (non-commissioned officers) present which despite my situation amused me greatly, though I tried not to smile. Mousey had noticed the fiasco was entertaining me and later asked what was so funny. I didn't tell him that I knew all along we shouldn't be there. We were taken back to camp, and then dispatched a few days later to Shepton Mallet in Somerset, which we knew, was where they sent you before discharge from the forces.

Looking back at those events; if we were being discharged, why did they feel the need to lock us up at all, was it just spite or resentment at having to let someone go? We hadn't actually done anything wrong; we were only terminating a contract.

In August, after serving seventy-six days in Shepton Mallet, we were sent back to the regimental barracks in civvies, to collect our discharge papers. The officer in charge of that detail must have liked the idea of messing us around some more, because he kept us waiting another four days without any explanation, before he summoned us to his office and gave us our papers. What did I get out of my time in the army? A little bit of back pay, a train ticket to my destination of choice, which was Southgate in North London to see Frances and they gave me my driving licence, which was like being given a gold bar.

Chapter 27

I arrived in Southgate to find Frances heavily pregnant and fairly near her time. We decided to wait for the baby to arrive, then get married. Paula was born a few weeks before Frances's seventeenth birthday. It wasn't unusual to see a young mother pushing a pram in the early sixties before the birth control pill was available. Boys would find it quite a challenge to walk into a chemist shop and request 'A pack of three' (condoms). Chemists were the only place you could buy them; assuming that you had the nerve to ask for them or the cash to pay for them. There was still a lot of prudish attitude around with regard to sexual freedom. Good girls didn't let boys go all the way until they were going steady or engaged; better yet, until they were married. At least, that's what the older generation thought! Most of the young dudes I knew had different ideas; the talk was often about which one of the girls was likely to let you.

With my newly issued Driving Licence I was taken on to drive a lorry for a scaffold hire company.

"What driving experience have you had?" was the interviewer's big question; to which the answer should have been "None," but I wasn't going to discuss my short comings as that wouldn't have secured me the job, so a large amount of 'Blagging' was needed as I told him about the ten-ton army truck I used to drive! Actually, I learnt to drive a sixty-ton Centurion battle tank and only watched as a manic sergeant drove me around in a Land Rover on Salisbury Plains, nearly turning the vehicle over several times, while I tried to operate the radio in the back as we played war games, does that count?

The first time I took a load out with the scaffold lorry I almost demolished a bus shelter while negotiating a corner. My lack of experience became immediately obvious as I hadn't reckoned on the length of the vehicle behind me, still; lucky no one saw me, so I drove on and learnt from the experience, soon getting quite adept at negotiating small alley ways and cul-de-sacs around London and the suburbs while delivering scaffolding to the fitters. Pity was that when the weather turned to winter, not so many builders were working outside. Consequently, scaffolding wasn't needed as much and one week before Christmas 1964, the last man to be taken on; who was me; got the sack. Not long afterwards, when I was working for a different company; while driving past the scaffold yard one day, just musing to myself about how unkind they had been, giving me my cards so close to Christmas, I noticed that the whole place had been destroyed by fire. I guess God doesn't pay back in pennies.

Residing in two small uninsulated rooms with a wife and baby in the attic of a house belonging to a couple from Spain and driving a lorry for a living was never going to suit me, even though my moonlighting activity collecting cardboard with the firm's lorry and selling it to a scrap paper merchant was earning some useful extra pennies. However, fate took a hand that summer when I found myself in more trouble. I was twenty-one years old, having had my twenty-first birthday just before being released from Shepton Mallet forces prison.

In 1965, despite being married, I still had an eye for the girls, but when one young lady took exception to my advances and landed a surprise hand across my cheek for being too advanced; with me being too quick of temper, I instinctively landed her one back. Well, that was stupid and obviously game over, so I beat a hasty retreat. Unfortunately, that wasn't the end of it, because she complained to the police. I didn't want my wife to know about my cheating, so I denied even being there, which only made matters worse. The court knew the truth of it and on hearing about my previous unsocial activities, sentenced me to three years open prison for assault. If I'd owned up to what really happened and let them know how sorry I was, they probably would have been more lenient with me, who knows.

Those events, traumatic as they were, turned out to be my saviour, as it gave me time to reflect on who I was and where I was going. Sometimes I think there is much we don't understand about ourselves and I can't help wondering if in some strange way I didn't orchestrate those events, drastic as it may seem; to gain some space for contemplation. It was like those other situations I've told you about; somewhere inside of me I knew what the outcome would be. I spent the next two years studying, taking my GCEs, (GCSE now), learning about graphic design and trying to become an artist. (Before the 'parole system' was introduced; the remission was one third for good behaviour.) I tried to keep my head down while in jail, but at one point trouble found me in the form of the cell block hard man and his cronies. My upbringing hadn't spared me any lessons in self-preservation; after all, it was an out of place reaction that got me banged up; so, I was able to deal with it appropriately. My ant agoniser's bruises were explained as him having fallen down the stairs! Nobody liked a 'Grass' in the nick so you never told tales.

During the last six months of my sentence; I was allowed out on leave several times in order to attend interviews for a place at Art College and was enrolled for a three-year Graphic Design course at East Ham Tech. The universities you see everywhere now, were mostly only colleges in the sixties; there has been a huge expansion in the number and class of education facilities, which is good; though maybe not so great, is the cost to our students of being educated by a service which at one time; you could easily get a grant for that you didn't have to pay back!

#

There is nothing more valuable than the freedom to make your own decisions, find your own time, come and go as you please, eat what you want, breath the free air around you. That list could go on forever, as I'm sure you know, songs have been written about it and anyone who's ever been banged up anywhere will tell you there's no price you can put on it. Don't take your freedom for granted, like the love of another, put it in your pocket, wear it on your chest, treasure it and look after it.

#

Frances went to live with her parents while waiting for me to return home from prison. She had two babies while I was away, the first was my son, whom she had been carrying when I got into trouble; the second was an accident that apparently came about with another man at a party. Don't forget, neither the birth control pill nor the morning after pill were available at the time. I had no grounds to complain about her going with another guy while I was away, but didn't feel able to handle three toddlers, one of whom wasn't mine. Her parents, Kath and Mac had lost a baby to leukaemia not many years before, they lived in the downstairs part of the house we were renting and were happy without any fuss or legalities to look after this lad and bring him up as their own. Kath unfortunately died quite young and Mac passed away not long after. I've been told they raised a well-balanced young man, though sadly, I have never met him.

Attending college, while working evenings and weekends for three years went by so quickly, I soon found myself in 1970 practicing graphics for real in an ad agency; no, not on a computer, we would have to wait nearly thirty years for those. This was all done by hand or with air brushes. I thought that the art in my portfolio was amazing, it certainly found me employment, but when I tried working alongside those seasoned artists; well, the word amateur comes to mind! College gives you the basic grounding, but doesn't prepare you for the real world; some of these artists were so slick they could produce the artwork almost to a photographic finish in no time at all. I know to watch and learn, but try as I might, I was always slower than the other artists and sure enough, the Art Director would quite often find fault with my work, sending it back to me for correction. I don't know if the other artists had the same problem, but I increasingly felt like a square peg in a round hole. However, when I moved to a different studio to work as a 'General Artist' preparing ads for the morning magazines and papers, the problem was solved. It was artwork that had to be produced at night with a print deadline for the early hours and with no art director to nag me which meant I was usually back home by 4am leaving time for some shut-eye and most importantly; allowing me to start working freelance during the day.

#

How many of you crave an adventure, something to take you away from the everyday norm? Most of you! Yes, I thought so, chances are though; it won't happen unless you make it. There has to be that little spark, that annoying itch you can't scratch; that voice inside daring you to take the challenge, trying to convince you of your invincibility. For me, it was the thought of making music. We had a folk music club at college where I used to take the guitar to sing a few songs, a couple of the hippier-type students went off with their guitars and hitchhiked overland to India, busking as they went. That seemed like a good adventure, but I wasn't sure how that could work with a wife and two children. Frances was very supportive of the idea and thought I should go on my own. I think it was more to do with making a marriage work. It seemed like we were discussing a separation but not actually separating, just taking a break from each other. Then again perhaps my upbringing had just left me with restless feet and Frances was intuitive enough to understand that. Anyway; this idiot went for it, catching a train to Dover and travelling on the ferry to Calais as a foot passenger with absolutely no plan and very little money or luggage except for my guitar. I must have walked halfway to Paris along the N1 (at least it seemed like it) before an English couple in a Mini Cooper stopped and gave me a ride the rest of the way. I had called into a café for a drink; when I went back out to the road; an elderly Frenchman caught me in conversation, though I couldn't understand much of what he said except when he pointed out the English driver's headlights coming down the road, because they were bright white and the French were driving on yellow headlights at the time. He was exploding with

"Ha englaise, regarde ca, englaise ha".

I had no trouble understanding his contempt and was extremely grateful when the vehicle stopped to give me a lift. The next summer, 1972, I went back to France with the family in a van that I had converted in to a camper.

When we saw a lone hitchhiker on that same stretch of road, I remembered the lift given to me the year before, so I took pity on him and picked him up. He was a French Canadian; we took him all the way to Paris. He kept the kids amused for a while, his accent was fascinating and he told them some funny stories, but when we got to the middle of the city, he decided that he wanted to stay with us as he didn't know anybody in Paris. We wanted to find somewhere quiet to bed down for the night so while I cruised around looking for a likely place to park and sleep, Frances and I were trying to persuade him that it was time to leave us, maybe go and find himself a hotel and make his own way to where ever he was going. After about a half hour of trying to get rid of him, it was getting late, I had no idea where we were and pulled up in what must have been some kind of red-light district. A kerfuffle immediately started outside the camper when some of the men hanging about, who had obviously had too much wine, noticed that we were English. The hitchhiker jumped out of the camper; supposedly to save us, being a French Canadian he seemed to know what the fuss was about (I didn't have a clue) then he surprised us even more by producing a small silver pistol from under his coat, and brandishing it at the crowd that had gathered. That just made matters worse with some of the more drunk Frenchmen shouting and waving their arms around in the air trying to get at him. When I saw the blue light of a gendarme car coming down the road behind us; I quickly slid the side door of the camper shut and pulled discreetly away, heading off to find a quieter street to park in for the night.

My little solo adventure the year before had lasted precisely five days; I did do some busking and was given a few much-needed

Francs by passers-by. Fontainebleau was as far south as I got having met up with a couple of girls who were on a camping holiday. We shared an evening camp meal, a nice conversation and some music, but I had to sleep outside their tent in my sleeping bag as I didn't own a tent of my own. In the morning my face was completely swollen from mosquito bites; which left me in a state of embarrassment about my looks; so, I didn't bother to wake the girls. I quietly had some breakfast on my own, sneaking off when I'd finished just as a disappointed sleepy female head popped itself out of the tent flap. I called back a hasty "Sorry I have to go" and made my way to the station, having made up my mind that being eaten by insects at night was a definite no no and that 'Home is where the heart is.' The journey back to London took two days, but the delight in young Paula and Trevor's eyes when their daddy walked through the door was something to be remembered.

#

Back in London, I soon picked up some freelance artwork, but the time between completing the work for a client and getting paid sometimes didn't match up, which often left us short of money, so I started wheeling and dealing second hand cars as well, using the estate car park where we lived to park any spare vehicles that I had bought. This involved a weekly trip to various car auctions hunting for that elusive bargain. More often than not, I would end up with a 'banger' that needed a lot of bodging and touching up before it was resell able. I didn't have a car of my own so I would drive around in whatever car I'd picked up from the auctions until it was sold. Once I sold an Austin 1100 to a chap 'as seen' who rang me up a week later complaining that the engine had dropped out of it! I ask you! What do you suppose he'd been getting up to with that car? No, I didn't give him his money back; the car was fine when it left me. I didn't hear any more about it. All kinds of exotic vehicles passed my way, form American Buicks and Pontiacs to Mercedes, Healeys and a Jaguar XK150 which even in the 1960's was an aficionado's car; many of them were exported to the USA.

Apart from the money aspect of owning an early Jaguar XK I wouldn't like to drive one around, they were a heavy car and the brakes were reluctant to stop them quick enough, which I learnt when a little girl ran out from behind an ice cream van one afternoon as I was passing it. Luckily, I was aware of the potential danger, even so, though only doing 10 mph, I was unable to stop quick enough and the heavy chrome front bumper caught her leg, fracturing her tibia bone. An ambulance and the police attended the scene, where I was found to be without fault. When I went with the little girl's parents to visit her in hospital, she was thankfully, all smiles with her leg plastered up saying how silly she had been and she would be more careful next time. Some years later in the 90s, when I found a rotting XK120 Jaguar in a barn, I started a part time venture importing Jaguars and Healeys back to the UK from the States to renovate and sell on.

#

At the time in 1972, the family who lived next door to us in Southgate were looking to buy a cheap house out of London, not too far away, so it would be possible to easily commute back. They hoped to find something in Northants with a bit of land to start a smallholding. The dream of 'self-sufficient' living was a news item at the time; along with going to India to find oneself, it was a popular notion that we could attain 'The Good Life'; a phrase which spurned a TV programme shortly after, depicting a middle class couple attempting to make 'The Good Life' work in suburbia. We quite liked the idea and managed to acquire a large collection of books extoling and explaining the subject. Feeling that I was now an expert, I decided to follow the neighbour's example and go house hunting in Northants.

One Saturday morning in March we drove up the M1 to look at a rundown property which was advertised at £2000 in a quiet rural village not far from the market town of Wellingborough. I was driving a rather flash American style Mercedes that I had bought at the car auction. We were a bit short of cash, so Frances went into the village post office to cash a £4 Giro cheque which was her unemployment benefit as she had lost her job.

The estate agent was based in Wellingborough, so that is where we headed after viewing the property, to make an offer on it. The country roads were nice and quiet, as you would expect in 1972, (there being a lot less cars on our roads than today, with many families not even owning one) but I did notice a rather tatty little red minivan behind me with two men sitting in the front seats as I negotiated the five miles of winding narrow road to Wellingborough.

The minivan was right behind us when we encountered a Saturday morning traffic jam as we entered the town, there was a hold up on both sides of the road so we had no choice but to sit and wait. The cars going out of town on the other side of the road were creeping past us, Frances was trying to amuse the children and keep them quiet, when all of a sudden four men hurriedly got out of a car that was heading out of town and came straight over to our Mercedes positioning themselves all around us. Thinking we were being hijacked for the car, I pushed the lock down on the driver's door, but we didn't have central locking like you do on a modern car so the man on the other side was able to throw open the passenger door shouting

"Police, get out of the vehicle!"

In the rear view mirror I noticed the minivan that was behind us had both its doors wide open and its occupants had jumped out of it, presumably, to help us, but in fact both of these men seemed to be a part of whatever was going on, which I realised when one of them threw open the rear door, causing the children to start screaming and then proceeded to try and push me out of the way to unlock the driver's door. Meanwhile, the man at the passenger door had produced what he proclaimed in a loud voice was a police warrant card and was flashing it around at us. As if we weren't all terrified enough, at that point the man on my side of the car pulled back his jacket to show me that he was wearing a pistol underneath it. He was shouting "Out of the car, out of the car!" as he gesticulated as if to pull the gun from its holster. So, I got out and was manhandled over to the pavement where one of them searched me and another pulled my hands behind my back to handcuff me.

Meanwhile I noticed that a uniformed police officer had arrived on the scene and was quizzing one of the men, they had a brief exchange then he left. Up until that moment, we had no idea who these men were or what they could possibly want with a young couple minding their own business, who had two small children travelling with them in a car.

It now became obvious that these men were indeed members of the police force in disguise. The traffic in front of the car which the men had got out of on the other side of the road had cleared away as had the traffic in front of our car, but there was still a queue of cars behind both vehicles which was being held up now by drivers wanting to see what was going on. One of the policemen was frantically waving at cars to move along past the scene, I have no doubt that because he was in scruffy plain clothes, like the rest of these officers, the other drivers were as confused as us. Then we were ushered across the road and made to get into a police van that had somehow managed to squeeze past everything, partially shoving pedestrian observers aside as it drove on the pavement to reach us. That was when I noticed the open boot of the other car these brave men were using, strapped inside of which were some more guns. No, it's true; our secret police were armed then, even though we didn't know it; of course, it's a lot more obvious in our modern world.

The whole fiasco ended about two hours later, but not after more shenanigans at the local police station where I was only saved from being locked in a cell by Paula and Trevor's howls and screams of terror at the thought of losing their dad. The officers relented and left a woman police officer to keep an eye on us while they did whatever checks they do on people they suspect of crimes. Eventually there were apologies from the policeman in charge as they gave us back the Mercedes and let us go.

Two weeks later we even got a formal letter of apology from the chief of police. It seems the post mistress at that village post office had nothing better to do than to ring the police about this doubtful looking family whom she'd never seen in the village before, who came into her post office and cashed a post office giro cheque, then drove off in an expensive looking American car. She even gave the police the registration number. The police, being on high alert because of the Irish Troubles which had kicked off not long before, were taking no chances and responded appropriately, so they said.

Chapter 28

It wasn't long before my itchy feet were looking for another adventure. Our neighbours, like us had failed in their self-sufficiency attempts and now seemed hooked on the idea of making a fresh start in Australia. I'd learnt my lesson about going off half-cocked, with the overland to India thing and this seemed like a good idea, so once again I put a lot of effort into research and preparation. At that time, in 1973, Australia allowed British nationals to enter the country, no visa, you just needed to get there and be able to support yourself. To that end, we sold pretty much everything out of our house, furniture, bicycles, tools, our children's toys, the TV, record player, pots, pans, we even found the dog a new home and packed the rest of our personal belongings into tea chests which we took to the docks to be shipped to us in Perth Australia, they would take six weeks to get there.

We got together enough money to buy the cheapest tickets for a family of four to Sydney Australia, which was a jet/ship journey, flying to Singapore then a week later getting a ship to Sydney.

Two evenings before flying off we took my dad and Bertha out for a fancy meal at a dinner dance venue beside the River Thames in Maidenhead, not so much as a treat, but more to say goodbye and to end an era. The cabaret was Anita Harris, she had a wonderful voice and watching the five piece band playing, was when I made a resolve to become a professional musician myself, I had no idea how, but I could sing and play the guitar, so the thought of it went onto the back burner in my head, I would look for an opportunity.

We almost missed the boarding time for our flight at Heathrow Airport because my dad insisted on driving the four of us and our luggage to the airport in a beat-up old Bedford van that I had bought him from the car auction. That was a first; not the van; I mean him driving us somewhere. I bet we'd made him feel guilty about his past lack of fatherliness by taking him out for a meal. The last time I rode anything with him was that motorbike he arrived on when visiting me at boarding school.

I had always thought of him as a master of the road, but at fifty-nine years old he was a menace of the road. He got lost twice, had to retrace where he'd driven to find the correct roads (no satnavs in 1973) we nearly hit a bus, mounted the kerb several times and came close to turning the van over while going around corners. The squealing of tyres, squeaking of brakes and crunching of gears became familiar sounds on that two-hour long drive that should only have taken about one hour. I think Frances needed a clean pair of knickers when we finally arrived at the airport, both the kids had spent the entire trip with white knuckles gripping on to the seat backs and I probably grew a few grey hairs. The wearing of seat belts was not a requirement in 1973, not that there were any in that old Bedford van.

The Boeing 747 jumbo jet taking us to Singapore had a stopover in Aden for refuelling. Because there was a small civil war going on, the passengers were led to the airport terminal via what we were told was an air-conditioned bullet-proof tunnel type of walkway, we could actually hear gunfire somewhere in the distance. None of it affected our flight and some hours later we arrived in Singapore stepping out of the aeroplane to be greeted unexpectedly by what felt like a blanket a warm, damp heat being thrown over us; it was wonderful. The skies did open up once while we were there, sending down torrents of warm rain that soaked you in just a few seconds, but then your clothes dried off in no time at all in the tropical heat.

Having spent a week exploring Singapore we went to board the ship which would take us to Sydney. Looking up at her from the docks, we were dismayed to be seeing a rusty disappointment. She seemed big but not nearly as big as I'd expected, she certainly wasn't the *Queen Mary*. We would be on her for a week, during which time I would win the singing competition, Frances would win the bingo, which was lucky for us, because at the time, we had run out of money. Then we would all be violently sick when the boat hit a major storm, with a thirty-foot swell, around the Australian Bight. Having been previously lulled into a false sense of security while cruising down an Indian Ocean which was wave less and looked more like glass.

As the wind and waves threw the ship about you would hear the ship's propeller whirring each time it came out of the water. It was pretty scary to watch the swimming pool empty itself like a bucket full of water being thrown around as the ship was tossed about by those enormous waves.

We docked in Melbourne before going on to Sydney, there was very little in the way of customs or immigration checking, for some reason the officials were more interested in looking at the palms of everyone's hands than their passports. At that time the Australian government was still using the 'White Australia' policy, although, history tells us that it was being phased out.

When we reached Sydney the first job was to find some reasonably clean but cheap accommodation. It wasn't like the twenty-first century, where you can carefully plan, vet and book everything on line prior to leaving. In 1973, we travelled on trust and hope and that found us a room in a massive hotel which was run by The Salvation Army called 'The Peoples Palace' the demolition of which in the 1980s was part of a massive change to the Sydney street scene.

Having settled ourselves in, we went exploring and were surprised to see familiar store names like Woolworths and Marks & Spencer out there, on the other side of the world, while we hunted around for camping and survival equipment. Our plan was to use an estate car like a camper, while driving around Australia. With two adults and two young children there wouldn't be much room, so we bought a large steel chest for our belongings which we fixed to the roof of the car. The rear of the 'station wagon' was slightly larger than the average UK estate car; the four of us could sleep with a top and tail arrangement in the back after the seats had been folded down, it was a bit of a squash, but it worked quite well. We spent six weeks driving and living out of that car; covering 16,000 miles on what were, at the time, mostly dirt roads. The only metalled roads were the highway that took us a few hundred miles north from Sydney, a road in the middle of the country that took us to Alice Springs, much of which got washed away in the rainy season and a brand new highway, which ran all the way down the west coast from Broome to Perth, nearly 1500 miles.

A lot of the dirt roads were either rock or red sandy earth which had been formed in to ruts by the weather and by the 'road trains'. (These were huge lorries that could pull as many as six trailers.) It is best to drive at over fifty-five miles per hour on those dirt roads, so that the vehicle only travels on the tops of the ruts and not up and down like on speed humps. Lack of steering control is a problem at that speed on a dirt road, but the roads are straight and meeting another vehicle was fairly rare. We only got two flat tyres the whole trip, one of which was shredded, so we replaced it with the spare, but we only had one spare and there were no garages for hundreds of miles, so when we got a second puncture and needed to remove the inner tube to repair it, we had no tools to take the tyre off the rim. There we were, on the Great Northern Highway, listening to the silence, looking at the Indian Ocean, not another living soul for a hundred miles or more, just the Australian bush. We were waiting and hoping for another traveller to come along the road who with luck, would be carrying the necessary tool.

Then in the very far off distance we heard the moan of a truck engine, the highway was straight, stretching out as far as the eye could see, undulating up and down with the terrain. We could hear a truck, but we couldn't see it; then we caught a glimpse of sunlight flashing on metal and could make out what we knew would be a road train on the horizon. Then it disappeared from sight as it went down a dip in the undulating terrain, then it appeared again as it came up a rise, then it disappeared, then it appeared, it kept appearing and disappearing for about fifteen minutes almost like we were watching a mirage. The only sense to tell us that it was real was the sound of it getting louder each time it reappeared as it got nearer. When the driver was close enough to spot us, about half a mile away, we waved frantically to catch his attention. Yes, he'd seen us and was going to stop; the engine decelerated, the air brakes hissed and hissed, the wheels squealed and rumbled and he finally came to a halt, fifty yards further on. Those road trains must weigh a bit and with the five huge trailers being towed along, must have taken a lot of stopping.

I had taken our wheel off and just needed a tool to break the bead of the tyre from the rim in order to remove the inner tube. (Thank heaven for the tubeless tyres we have now!) The road train I learnt has its own work shop behind the driver's cab and this chap had a spare tool which he lent us just in case we got another puncture. After he had helped fix our punctured inner tube, we shared a mug of tea with him, then he gave us his address in Perth so that we could return his tool when we were down that way (about a thousand miles away). How trusting was that? Well that truck driver got us out of trouble and we did subsequently look him up a month later to return the tool and have dinner with his family.

With the best of intentions, we decided to settle down in Perth and moved into a small block of flats in Mosman Park. Both Frances and I found jobs straight away and the kids started a new school. Things were going great till I lost my job working as a graphic artist; it seems the politics of employment hadn't changed at all, only the location. Coincidentally, at about the same time, a band I joined who had split up from their singer decided to take him back again, so they kicked me out. Fair enough; I picked myself up and found another band to work with, I also got started as a self-employed decorator, there were a lot of new buildings going up, so sub contract work was plentiful. I was given a job decorating five newly built houses, but there was too much work for one man to do and my funds didn't run to employing a painter, so Frances gave up her job to come and work with me. We bought gallons of the required paint and other materials, planning to finish the first house, then invoice the contractor to get some money back while we carried on with the second property. We had completed all three bedrooms upstairs, as well as the stairwell and were working on the lounge when the contractor turned up at the job. He looked at all the work we had completed and was happy with the standard of it. Then he noticed my wife painting the ceiling in the lounge; that was when the shit hit the fan.

"What's a Sheila doing on the job?" he demanded.

I told him it was my wife.

"Oh! No, it isn't" he retorted "We don't have Sheila's doing a man's work here; either get her off the job or you can f__ck off and don't come back."

My choice was obvious, but to make matters worse he was refusing to pay for the work we had completed or the materials we had bought for the job.

"I'll be back in an hour and you'd better be gone with her," was his answer.

Nice man eh?! My bit of vengeance before we drove away was to accidentally empty three gallons of paint everywhere. Oops! Well: we wouldn't be needing it.

Three knock backs in six months was never going to get me down, I was having fun some evenings singing in beer gardens and clubs with the band; we even played at a few functions. Buying and selling second hand cars was a flop as was trying to sell my paintings, so I gave that up deciding to try second hand furniture instead, but that only lost money too, finally, I answered an ad in the newspaper. Someone was looking for a person to take over a milk round. How hard can that be; didn't I used to help the milkman at weekends when I was fifteen? No money was needed; the chap even gave me the Toyota milk truck to treat as my own while I was doing the round, which had to be done at night, because there was a bylaw forbidding milk floats to operate during the day; they had to be off the road by 8 am in the morning. Ok that doesn't sound so bad, we had a torch and there must be streetlights surely? There had to be a rub, who hands over a readymade income on a plate, just like that?

Well, at first it looked like this chap did. We started going to the dairy to pick up a truck load of milk at ten o'clock each evening after we'd made sure the kids were settled down and asleep. (They were only nine and ten years old and had settled into Australia really well; even coming home each day from school with no shoes on their feet.) I know what you will be thinking; "Did you leave them on their own all night?"

Well; yes, we did; can't imagine that now, can you? Anyway, in order to get the milk distribution finished by 8 am we had to drive round deserted night time streets and run to every house; delivering fresh milk and collecting the empty bottles; we were like a couple of whirlwinds. Then, in the morning we got home, sorted the kids out for school and went to bed ourselves just like any other night worker.

In Australia everything bites; spiders, snakes, mosquitoes and lots of them come out at night, especially spiders who love to weave huge webs across people's porches and verandas to catch their dinner in. Now when you are running around in the dark looking for empty milk bottles to collect and replace with the full ones that you are carrying, it is really useful to have the odd street light nearby to send glistening rays of light out that reflect on those empty bottles and the silky spider's webs which you would otherwise probably run into. That same light also lets you see the redback spider, who will have made a nest in the empty milk bottle which you are about to pick up. The easiest way to pick up those bottles is to stick your fingers in the open bottle tops which is where Mrs Redback will be waiting for her dinner. Oh yes, they bite! I once nearly picked up a Dugite snake in the dark, thinking it was a small stick and they bite as well.

What we had no knowledge of, was the local council's agenda to shut off all street lighting at 11.30 pm each evening to save electricity. A couple of months after we started the milk round, we found ourselves in pitch darkness on the streets at night. Now we knew what the catch was with the free milk round, but we still tried to carry on with the milk deliveries, even though it became nigh impossible to complete by 8 am in the morning, as it took so much longer to find where people had left their empties and to check for spiders. We knew that we were going to have to give this nice little earner up.

We had managed to get a mortgage for a building plot in Maida Vale and were having a house, that I had designed erected on it. The building development firm was run by two guys, who were also English, they had asked me to design several houses for them as part of the financial arrangement we came to. Our house had been started and we were getting excited at the thought of having a more permanent home than the ones we had been renting. The walls were up, but building came to a halt without a roof. It turned out that the developers had run out of money, so I ordered the roof tiles myself from the tile manufacturer paying for them out of our profits on the milk round, I also financed the men to fix them in place, so we had a roof. Then work on our house stopped again. Realising that we had been conned; I had a massive row with those two Englishmen who called themselves house developers and one of them subsequently did a moonlight (disappeared) while the other chap was reported to have had a mental breakdown. Anyway, we'd had enough of disappointments and decided in 1974 to dump the milk round, abandon the half-built house and head back to the UK. True, we had to pull a few stunts ourselves to finance that return trip at short notice, but we managed to package our personal belonging up, take them to a shipping line and get a flight back to Heathrow in not too many days. End of Australian adventure, I don't regret it.

Chapter 29

Back in the UK we used our last £200 to buy an old car and pay for one month's rent on a house. My wife found herself a job and I was offered a position as a studio manager, but decided not to take it; instead, I would concentrate on becoming a full-time musician, or at least, to earn a living in the music business. An ad in the local paper for guitar students was immediately fruitful, as was an ad in the music press asking for work as a singer/guitarist. I turned our dining room into a music studio and attended two or three auditions which gained me some work.

My first two students turned out to be 'punk rockers', both of these lads being teenagers, were sporting brightly coloured sculptured hair on their heads, chains hanging from their duffle coats and large Doc Marten boots on their feet. They had arrived at the house early and were standing out in the street with their electric guitars waiting for me, when Frances and I returned on foot from the shops.

This was the early days of punk and we had never seen a display quite like it. Teaching was a new venture for me, though I'd done a lot of study and prepared myself, in my head I hadn't made any allowance for the fact that we are not all the same. Consequently, the thought of teaching these two punk rockers who were waiting outside my house expectantly, was a little scary; how could I be so naïve?

Frances was apprehensive about having these two aggressive looking lads in the house and put a final nail in the coffin when she urged me to walk on round the block with her, hoping that they would have given up and left by the time we returned; which they had. Now that; is one of those errors of judgement I have never forgotten, or forgiven myself for. 'You can't judge a book by its cover'. I had a class full of like youngsters in the 80s who were most receptive to gaining knowledge and taught me a thing or two in return about their music and fashions, which reminds one that 'To teach is to learn.'

Frances and I split up that year, 1974, for six months when she moved out, leaving me to look after the kids who were nine and ten years old. I established myself as a music teacher with quite a few private pupils, a peripatetic post in a secondary school and two adult classes at evening school plus a regular job singing in front of a trio who were the resident band in a pub two evenings a week. Once again, Paula and Trevor had to be left on their own sometimes, just like when we were in Australia. I was there at breakfast and other meals, for coming and going to school and for bedtimes, but I had to apprehensively leave them alone in the evenings after I had put them to bed when I went out to play a gig with the band. Can you imagine that nowadays, gosh the council would probably have a fit and remove your kids in a flash?

By the end of the year I had formulated a plan which Frances was eager to be part of, so she returned home. House prices had just started to increase, a phenomenon which has led to the staggering property prices we see in the twenty-first century. Though interest rates were high at around 13%, I knew that if we fiddled the figures for work income and our savings, we could get a mortgage on a semidetached house needing some improvement; do the work and sell it on; thus gaining some capital which was needed to open a music shop.

The hoped-for house purchase was a property just in the next street that I had my eye on. Supply and demand is the catalyst driving enterprise and in 1975, the competition for a bargain was stiff which resulted in the term 'gazumping' being coined, but we were fortunate in that the house owners had been elderly and passed away leaving a home that needed a lot more work than most folk were willing to undertake and it didn't have off street parking. Here is where being a musician, having a lot of day time free, put me at an advantage where the work was concerned. We bought it, a three-bedroom semi in Friern Barnet, North London for... wait for it... £12,500. Yes, you read that right; I wonder what it's worth now, £600,000? Perhaps we should have just sat tight! No challenges in that though.

I'll just mention a couple of things about that house. You remember I wrote how the previous owners had been elderly and passed away; well, their thirty-something-year-old son and daughter went through all of what were probably these folk's life possessions taking anything they found useful, which is right, but leaving everything else that their parents had owned or collected scattered all over the house and garden. That included personal items like their mother's corsets and underwear and what were probably their dad's treasured tools and bits and bobs. Bank statements, passports, pension books, war medals, photos, it was the saddest most disrespectful thing you can imagine. You could tell from their dad's abandoned tools that he was a doer. I have retained some of his stuff in amongst my own, there is a tin in which he kept 'useful' bits and pieces, I feel like I knew him every time I pick that rusty old tin up looking for the odd useful screw or spring I might have stored in there.

Then there were the neighbours. The chap was a policeman, a dog handler; their name was Law. (Don't laugh!) That used to amuse me, especially when he banged on our front door at around 9.30 pm one evening laying down the law, telling me that I was making too much noise. What was I doing? Well, I was pulling tacks out of the staircase, the sound of which was travelling through the party wall. The houses were unusual in that they had halls adjoining. I thought he was just being pernickety as I was trying not to make too much noise. Funny thing was that later when we had the music shop, we couldn't park a car outside in the main road, so we used to park our Ford Capri around the corner near a house that was owned by a policeman. Someone tried to break into the car one night, setting off the alarm. This nice 'neighbour' called round to the shop the next day to ask us if we could do anything about our car alarm. I pointed out to him that it was needed to deter would be thieves. He replied that he didn't want to have to listen to our car being broken in to! Eee! There's now't like folk.

The house was renovated and back on the market by early spring 1976. Most of the work had gone quite smoothly until I hammered a pin into a lead water pipe that was buried deep in the bathroom wall. Lead piping is not used in houses anymore, but did you know that you could reseal a hole like that in lead pipe just by plugging it up. Well, anyway that's what I did; with a matchstick. The people who bought that house from us, never complained about water spurting out at them from the bathroom wall, which is what happened to me, so I'm guessing my repair held water!

#

The only way we could acquire shop premises was to rent them; so, with the house sold we found a property on the main road with self-contained living space upstairs that had a shop with store rooms downstairs. After we moved in we spent the first month decorating and shop fitting. Then I had to approach all the suppliers of musical paraphernalia for stock to fill the shop. We would need to have a large choice of everything, one guitar would have been no good, we needed many guitars and lots of different brands; the same rule applied to everything else in the shop.

Representatives from wholesale warehouses and musical instrument makers were eager to do business with us, only one or two suppliers worked on a 'proforma' basis (pay for goods before you get them) most of the companies were happy to have a pay monthly policy, which allowed us to stock the shop comprehensively. The credit arrangement was necessary because our cash flow was limited. Establishing a shop so that you had a regular flow of customers was going to take some time, but I had a trump card, which was to use the store room for guitar classes as I already had a steady stream of students. (and students need instruments and other music paraphernalia.) Also, my music career had moved up to playing at really swish dinner dance, cabaret venues where many of the guest cabaret acts were famous entertainers.

Our music shop was situated in a parade of shops; we had a Greek restaurant on one side of us and a launderette on the other side. We used to joke with the property insurance rep that we could get flooded by the launderette or burnt down by the restaurant.

We were woken up in the early hours one morning by fire sirens and someone banging on our front door. Ironically, there was a fire in the launderette; the street was blocked off by three fire tenders, the occupants of which had already unrolled countless miles of hose from their machines and were pumping gallons of water at the building. We had to evacuate our premises as fast as we could. Smoke from the fire was seeping through the walls into our premises. I had done fire drill in the army and at the Civil Defence with the Dales so I knew to keep calm and assure the family that we would be alright. Waking the kids up, grabbing clothes, blankets and anything else we could think of we made our escape down a stairwell which was full of thick black smoke that was actually hissing through the wall adjoining the launderette at some speed.

That wasn't the end of our drama, as one week after the insurance company had reinstated our premises from the smoke and water damage; we had the council round because there was a rat problem in the alley behind the shops which they had pinpointed as the fault of waste food bins left out by the restaurant. Exciting life having a shop!

We were also surprised one evening, while watching TV in the flat above the shop by a massive crash on the front of the building as someone carried out a smash and grab raid at about 10.pm on our shop, making off with several guitars before the alarms; which had a delayed action, went off and the police arrived. Nothing of any great value was stolen.

The police bought three guitars round a few days later, for us to identify; informing us that they had apprehended a suspect with them. We were unable to honestly say that they were ours, because someone had made a pretty good job of scratching out the registration numbers on all three guitars, so there was no way to identify them accurately. The detective who bought them round tried to badger me into saying the guitars were from our shop, but I sensed that he was just eager to get a conviction, as you can imagine, he was pushing the wrong guy; I stood my ground.

Chapter 30

The dream of 'self-sufficiency' had never really vanished and its crazy head sprung up again when we learnt of land being sold for $1 per acre in Paraguay, South America. Like Australia, there were no restrictions for us on entry into the country in 1977. I developed a sudden strong desire to see North America as well; we could tour there first and then travel overland to Paraguay to buy some acreage. This whole mad idea was being fuelled by those dramas taking place around us and our financial situation which was far from fluid. Stocking and fitting out the music shop had taken a great deal of money, a lot of which was on credit to various suppliers, any one of whom would only give us limited credit as a new venture, but when you added up several suppliers, that came to a lot of investment money. While we were able to pay all the monthly invoices, everything we earned was going straight out again, so we couldn't foresee a point at which we would be making a profit. In 1977 we decided to sell up and go follow that dream again.

Emptying a shop of all its contents is incredibly easy when you are practically giving everything away. A half-price sale will have the place overrun by vultures before you can say "Bargain!" Even before the doors open, that word 'Bargain' can create a queue that stretches to Scotland and back. We knew the score, having practically given away all that second hand furniture we collected together when we tried to start a second hand furniture enterprise in Australia. It took about two weeks to clear the flat and shop of all their contents, the only item left was a Hammond organ in the shop which we'd been asked to sell by a client and hadn't been able to.

Having done a moonlight from the shop, we flew off to Canada, leaving the UK behind with a stash of money in our boots on a dismally grey day in mid-April; arriving in Toronto to be greeted by a pleasant fourteen degrees of sunshine. Everything we owned was in our suitcases, we even took the dog; which was a rough Collie called Monty. (He was kept in a special cage in the aeroplane hold.) We bought him as a pup in Australia and were so impressed with him as a guard dog that we had flown him back to the UK with us in 1974 and then could only visit him every week for six months while he was in quarantine. Today we have certified rabies injections, microchipping, pet passports and veterinary certificates which have all helped to change how the pet movement rules work.

While in Toronto we bought a four berth Volkswagen Camper that was going to be our home for the next month or so while we drove to South America. At least that was the plan, until the American Embassy told us of a civil war that was raging in Central America and strongly advised against journeying there. Change of plan; head for Miami after touring the USA for a bit; sell the camper; get a flight down to Paraguay.

Arriving at Niagara Falls to enter the USA we encountered another small problem because we had no UK return address. We were led into the emigration office to be interviewed with regard our intentions in the U.S. The officials must have liked our faces as they let us continue with our journey having shortened our visa from six to three months. I don't suppose that would have made much difference if we had decided to stay in America; at that time, the problems modern governments are experiencing with illegal immigration hadn't reached such a crescendo and the States still had a fairly relaxed open-door policy, especially to Brits.

Monty was a natural guard dog, but as such he was a bit of a liability. So keen was he to look after his owners that he even became a threat to anyone walking within earshot of us whenever we had taken him out walking on Hampstead Heath. Leaving him to guard the camper in New York, where fire regulations meant that we had to leave our camper unlocked in car parks, put our mind at rest with regard to the safety of our possessions stored inside. Then when we were in Asunción Paraguay, the four-star hotel room we stayed in had no windows or locks on the doors, but we were pretty sure of our own furry black and white security arrangements when we went out. Monty wasn't always God's gift though; when we were in Upstate New York he took it upon himself to hunt a man who was bending over with his back to us rummaging in the boot of his car. The chap was about a hundred metres away in the camping area where we had spent the night. We were just having breakfast and momentarily distracted from watching him when Monty saw his prey. There had been no other travellers in the rest area all night, leading us to be lenient and not have the dog on a leash. We hadn't noticed another car arrive, then with horror I saw Monty halfway between us and the new arrival, he was crouched down creeping up hunting style on the bent over man who was just minding his own business. As soon as Monty heard me shout "No!" he was on his feet and into a full run, determined to complete his mission, lunging himself at the man's backside, there was no stopping him. I got to the scene in a flash, grabbing the dog's collar, pulling him away from his victim, It turned out lucky that Monty wasn't very good at attacking large bottoms as the only physical damage inflicted was a ripped pair of brightly coloured checked golfing trousers. The poor chap was badly shaken though and it took all of our diplomatic skills plus a $100 bill to calm him down. We bundled everything back into the Volkswagen and hit the freeway, putting some miles between us before there were any other 'legal' repercussions; although, that's another thing to have changed in our society; you would be biting your nails worrying about getting sued here in the twenty first century; we'd never heard of such a thing forty-odd years ago.

#

Monty would accompany us travelling more than half way round the world and be a good friend to have , but when we landed in Madrid on route back to the UK later that year, we were woken up to the fact that the import papers necessary to bring him back to the UK were not in place. The only thing for it was to leave him in the airport kennels while the official documents were obtained. So, we arranged for that internment to go ahead and were soon paged over the airport loud speaker system to attend the cargo area, where none of the staff were able to open the flight cage to let Monty out because he was being so aggressive and threatening to attack them. He came to me with no bother; he even sat and laid down quietly when I told him to. He was a well-trained dog normally, doing exactly what he was told; I think the flights and all the activity had upset him pretty badly. In the meantime, two of the airport security guards had turned up, one of them was a dog handler with an Alsatian guard dog on a chain lead. He looked Monty over and was impressed by his bearing and his attitude. The other man spoke good English and suggested that Monty would be a perfect dog to work with them patrolling the airport perimeter. I could see they were dog lovers by their own dog and by the way they handled Monty and I knew what the man had said to me was true, so after consulting with Frances and the kids, we said goodbye to Monty and let them take him to become a working dog.

#

After about a month of touring the USA we eventually arrived in Miami having drunk pure crushed apple juice from flagons bought at the road side in the Blue Ridge Mountains, broken down and been vanless for two days in Memphis, wondered at the poor housing in the Deep South where many African Americans were living in tin shacks and heard complaints from a couple of Texans in a diner because we were served more roast beef than them; the waitress having favoured us because we were from England!

On arriving in Miami, we took a wrong turn off the freeway and found ourselves in an estate of tenement housing suddenly surrounded by a large crowd of coloured people who were none too friendly when they saw us white folk invading their territory.

Things calmed down a bit when some of them realised that we were visitors who had lost their way. We soon caught on to the prejudice that was causing the situation and were quick to let the men who were nearest the camper know that we were visitors from England. The van had a Canadian registration so it wasn't hard to convince them; then there was smiles and chat all round. I hate to think how that would have turned out if we had been white Americans.

We had no trouble selling the camper in Miami for more than it cost us in Toronto, even though our travels had added 6000 miles to the clock. Flight tickets to Asunción were purchased and we were soon on the first leg of the trip south, landing in La Paz where there was another civil war raging. This was an overnight stop for refuelling and checks on the twelve-seater plane that was our transport. It was nice to meet an English sales rep on the flight who spoke Spanish because we had overlooked the importance of at least attaining a basic understanding of the language, which would prove to be a costly mistake when we tried to leave Paraguay.

It didn't take us long to discover a country full of poverty as we drove in the hire car on a dirt road down to The Chaco, which was the area in western Paraguay where land was being sold off. Today the area is part of the country that is subject to rapid deforestation. We in the West complain, but a third world country like Paraguay relies heavily on agriculture to survive; it's hard to know how we humans can strike the best balance between our requirements and Mother Nature.

The people we saw and met were obviously poor folk, but were always very friendly and helpful towards us. They are a dual language country, where finding ways to communicate can be challenging. We found that their native tongue is called Guarani, as is the currency, so our Spanish phrase book became fairly useless away from the capital city of Asunción. Not many of the houses we saw on the roads out of town had any windows or doors, they were mostly what you might call adobe brick huts. There is an obvious difference between the few rich and the many poor. We couldn't imagine ourselves making a life there, especially for the kids, but hey! The adventure and life learning experience were fun. So it was back to the world we knew, but not until we had been conned into paying twice the proper rate for a taxi from our hotel to the airport; then having got there, we needed to bribe an airport official to let us board the one flight out of Asunción on that day. Problems that could probably have been negotiated better if we'd learnt some Spanish.

#

Back in the UK after just six weeks, we didn't dare show our faces in London; instead we bought a Rover 95, headed to York, couldn't afford the cost of property rental there, got lost and ended up in Leeds; where we rented a house with our last pennies. The first week we were living in Leeds, Frances got a job with an estate agent, I sold a camera and some other bits to get cash, for food and essentials, found a band to work with and started taking on guitar students, plus we got Paula and Trevor straight back into school. I'm not sure that in today's job and housing market you could achieve these things so easily, or maybe it was just our enthusiasm that caused us to survive. Looking back, I seem to have spent a lot of time chasing my tail, but then you can't put a value on life experience, can you?

Working with a band, entertaining folk in working men's clubs around the North of England was a different experience; you have to be an act, not just background music. These audiences have seen it all and have probably heard all the jokes as well, so you had better be on your toes. No forgetting your words or chords, no amateurs setting up on stage, be professional, leave them wanting more, then if the agent likes you, he will give you more work and hopefully, more lucrative bookings. After a while I found that I could earn more money working as a solo artist; this was before backing tracks became the norm. Most of the clubs had their own resident organist and drummer; all you needed to take along to the gig with you were your guitar and your dots (music for the musicians to play) plus something flashy to change into while you were on stage. If you were lucky the resident band could read music otherwise, they just blagged it and played by ear; hey presto, instant band. What a pity that way of life has all but disappeared with so many clubs closing down, having become unviable for various reasons; some political, some social. The clientele has changed with adjustments to the available jobs and there is a new generation who have a different perspective on entertainment. Fashions don't stay the same, people move around and young folk move away to find work elsewhere. The altered rules on drinking and smoking (Crikey! Do you remember smoke filled rooms where you couldn't see as far as the back wall for smog?) have also contributed to the demise of club land. We have open mike nights, quiz nights and karaoke nights now, anyone can have a go, the worlds full Frank Sinatras and Shirley Basseys. (This is not a bad thing.) Besides the public entertain themselves for nothing and what else boosts your ego more than being a star, either the quiz winner or the entertainer? So, landlords quite often don't need to pay money out for a bunch of musicians to do the job.

That's my 'rant' finished!

#

I'll just tell you a bit about the Webster's Great Northern Talent Contest that caught my attention in 1979. Having failed an audition for ITV's *New Faces* in 1974 where I went along for it completely unprepared, I made sure that I was properly suited and booted with plenty of practice behind me before entering the Webster's competition. As you would expect, there were some brilliant acts in the running for the first prize of £1000. There were several heats and elimination processes culminating in a grand finale in Leeds which I managed to win through to. Do you chew your nails when you are nervous, well, the finals of any competition must be nail biting, however, I resisted the temptation and as I told you earlier; became the winner of that competition. Not only was the cash prize very useful as Frances and I had split up (again) leaving me to look after two young teenagers and a mortgage, but a phone call from an agent the next day asking if I would be interested in joining a hit recording band called *The Casuals* was very exciting.

You know; everybody is supposed to have fifteen minutes of fame, well, that was mine. I went along, met the band, played at a lot of fancy venues with them, which was fun because the audiences always knew who the band were and had come to see them; earned plenty of pennies doing it, but then after a while I got fed up of sitting in dressing rooms, as most of the sets we did were at 11 or 12 pm and you needed to be at the venue much earlier in the day to set up the equipment and do sound checks. It became normal to be waiting hours to go on stage while watching the drummer getting drunk. (He died of liver failure some years later.) They were a very good band but they had to play the same old numbers at every gig; it was what the crowd expected of them. You can guess the rest; I was going back to being a solo entertainer. I still do gigs but only for functions if I'm asked to play. Since leaving *The Casuals* I have worked with other bands and for a few years around 2003, with a girl singer as a duo which was probably the most rewarding experience musically and I must admit that I miss the harmony work. People would often approach us and comment on a song we had performed with remarks like "You made the hairs stand up on the back of my neck." I can't think of anything nicer than being able to touch someone with your music like that.

#

Can I talk about some affairs of the heart now?

Rosalyn had been my first love as a lost eleven-year-old in boarding school; I mean; could you call it love, that infatuation with the opposite sex? I had never really been around girls before, except for maybe the Dutch girl in infant school who had me thinking erotic thoughts which left me innocently playing with myself. Oh! Bertha caught me doing that and strapped a pair of those wire pan cleaners to my hands at night in an attempt to deter me from the activity. Actually; it just made my thoughts more erotic.

Frances was probably my first real love, for a few weeks anyway. Well, I used to get bored easily and a new conquest was always around the corner. I have to admit to a scenario that followed me right through the relationship; first one secret affair and then another. Do you know; I think I must have been fucked up as a lad. What on earth could possibly be wrong with forever kind of love, with one man one woman? No; it can come and go like the weather; like Alison who was in the audience while accompanying another artiste who was on the bill at a Country and Western night. She caught my eye while I was singing, then came to sit with me during my break as the bingo was being drawn. She was so young and beautiful and obviously attracted to me; I fell in love all over again, though not like before, this was adult love, this was me at thirty-six years old. I remember Frances once accusing me of being 'besotted' with her; I thought how astute that was, just like a woman.

Alison and I tried to make a go of it by moving in to a flat together; it lasted one week before I moved back to live with Frances in a relationship that had become more off than on, but hinged around us having two children. As you know, we were eventually divorced; while Alison on the other hand, had been on the pill, but came off it without telling me; got pregnant and had our baby girl. I felt a marriage with her would be a mistake; it's funny how you can be in love with someone and yet be so different. Alison eventually met and married another guy and they asked for my permission to officially adopt our daughter. That hurt; that hurt a lot, but letting them go ahead as a couple was the only sensible thing I could do. Besides, they were living in Scotland, at the time, where the law would have allowed them to go ahead without my permission anyway.

Time heals and life moves on; Ruth came into my life just before Trevor and I moved to Knaresborough in 1982; she came to learn the guitar. Normally I wouldn't dream of dating a student of mine but I was drawn to her and seemed to spend a lot of time gazing into her large green eyes while discussing quarter notes and quavers and secretly admiring her breasts. As I got to know her, I was learning what a down to earth person she was, very calculating and really careful; not the type of person like myself, who would take risks; I was attracted by the safety of that. Ruth on the other hand was discovering what an upfront have a go type of guy I am and was attracted to what was quite possibly her opposite. Of course we got together, much to the consternation of her parents who hated the idea of their daughter going with a divorcee who was not only seventeen years older than their daughter but who already had two teenage children.

Chapter 31

I don't know how many of you have never met a parent or maybe both of your parents, it's not the same as wondering who your great grandad was or some other distant relative; this is someone who should have been there with you, loving and guiding you every day. I grew up dreaming of what my mum might be like. I imagined her as a brunette, good looking, of average height, clever, chatty and slim. I also imagined myself going back home to Cornwall and finding her there one day. I knew absolutely nothing about my mother; if you had asked my dad anything about his ex-wife or his past life, the answer would be something like, "I don't want to talk about any of that lad, it's best forgotten, it's all in the past now",

Well I may have imagined myself going to look for my mother, but at thirty-eight years old, I never had; at least not until Ruth; who was a nurse, had one of her work associates in 1982 give her the loan of a flat they owned in Cornwall for her two week holiday.

Do you know, it was as easy as falling off a log to find my mother and her family, even though I was only following my instincts, not really having any idea what to do. We went down to the Lizard, where I was born, asked in the local pub to see if anyone knew the name, the landlord of the pub had been there forever and knew the family, he was even in touch with my mum's sister Betty, who lived in Marazion. He phoned her up, she came straight along to the Lizard to meet me, then she rang my mum who was living and working as a singer in London. Her name was Ruby; she came down on the train the next day to meet her son whom she hadn't seen for thirty-six years. It also turned out that I had a whole other family on her side who I had never met. So finally, a face put to an imagining. Blonde, not brunette, good looking, stylishly dressed, not chatty, a loner very much living in her own thoughts, in fact she seemed quite a sad soul. How strange to think of all the years I spent living in and around London, never knowing that my mother was not many miles away. I have often wondered if my dad had known where she was.

Though I saw her a few times over the years after that first meeting and she always sent me Christmas and Birthday cards; I never got to know her, even though we did talk on the phone sometimes and on the few occasions when I did get to Cornwall to see her, we would share nothing more than the time of day and a cup of tea before she tired of my company and asked, "Will you be leaving now?"

Despite the brief exchanges, thirty-six years of never knowing my mother was put to rest for me, I often wonder if she had also found peace with the subject, after all, isn't motherhood supposed to be a basic instinct? And I don't understand how a mother can be so indifferent. In the end, I was the last person to speak to her before she passed away in 2015, aged ninety-six. It was on the phone, Yorkshire to Cornwall as usual and her parting words to me were, "Goodbye, don't call again."

Was she being unkind? I don't know; she didn't have dementia; I think she must have been suffering some pain because she'd asked to be sent home from hospital to die, owing to being in renal failure. All I have left of my mum is an old 1945 photograph of her at the family home in Cornwall with me in a pram and some wonderful oil paintings that she did and then sent to me, of the sea, of people camping on a cliff and some cottages with roses round the door and children playing in the garden.

She had been married four times, the first marriage was to my dad and I'm not surprised that she left him, with her being such an independent soul. Ruby's second husband was stabbed to death in a pub, her third husband died suddenly, of a brain tumour and her fourth husband really did come down with a serious case of dementia, passing away just weeks after Ruby. Hey; if the left one doesn't get you, the right one will. Happy days.

Chapter 32

Eighteen months after moving into the house in Knaresborough in 1982, it was back on the market producing enough cash to buy another house which in its turn was sold on a year later. Normally, you would move out of one house, straight into another that you had bought or maybe were going to rent, but in this case we had been unable to find a property that suited us so we were likely to be homeless or renting when our buyers took over their new house. It happened that one of my guitar students was an elderly priest and he very kindly let Ruth and I stay in the church house while we hunted for our next property. We are not Catholic, in fact we don't really attend any church, Father Theo was just a very nice man

#

Well, in 1986 we nearly ended up with a smallholding in North Wales to make an attempt at being self-sufficient, but on the occasion when I rang my dad to say "Hello" not having spoken to him for ten years, he was curious about what I was up to, then pretty negative at the thought of self-sufficiency saying

"Pie in the sky lad, pie in the sky".

He never could see me do a good thing, always being negative about my struggles in life, still it did make me think twice, causing Ruth and I to back out of the North Wales project at the last minute. I've never looked back or lived in an 'If only' world; except maybe a small regret somewhere in the back of my mind at dumping the music shop! You put your best foot forward and find a new challenge… life is an adventure.

The dilapidated cottage in North Yorkshire we found in 1986 instead of a smallholding in Wales was about 200 years old, made of cobbles with a tiled roof. From what we could see, no attempt to modernise it had ever taken place, the family who had owned it only used it as a getaway once or twice a year as they lived in Essex. Our furniture and belongings had been in storage while we were homeless; when it arrived at the cottage we re-stored most of it in an old barn that looked fairly dry which was part of the property, only moving things in to the house that were immediately needed so as to leave room inside it for doing the renovating. The services to the village didn't include gas, only electricity and water, the supply of which we had turned on by the utility providers.

Having moved in and feeling really pleased with ourselves at our acquisition, Ruth and I took the dog for a walk-in nearby woods that first April evening we were in the cottage. On returning home we caught site of an orange glow that was lighting up the evening sky ahead of us. I commented to Ruth that someone must be having a massive bonfire, but when we got in site of the cottage we had taken possession of not many hours before we were horrified to see that it was the source of the fire, with flames shooting up into the evening sky out of its roof. One of the neighbours had spotted the blaze and rung the fire brigade; she was standing on the other side of the road watching the flames eat our house away while waiting for them to arrive.

The nearest towns were both five miles away and both towns only having a part time fire service, meant that the first fire tender didn't arrive for at least forty minutes after the alarm was raised. In the end three fire tenders attended the scene. The firemen did their best to contain the blaze, but 200-year-old timbers are very dry and just love to disappear when attacked by flames. We were left with the remains of a cottage that included four walls and thankfully a couple of the ancient wooden beams that looked like they had been salvaged at some point from a ship and now supported the remains of the upstairs two bedrooms. Of course, they were both badly charred but did eventually clean up quite nicely.

You would be foolish if when buying a house, you didn't take out some insurance; of course, we did. Unlike my grandparents, who were uninsured when their bakery was burnt down in America; they lost everything. The insurance investigators concluded that there had been an electrical fault in our cottage wiring which caused a short circuit and started a fire. Subsequently, because the woodwork was so old and dry; it all went up like a match.

Ruth and I bought an old two-berth caravan, which we manhandled on to the overgrown and neglected cottage garden to live in while we rebuilt the cottage. Scaffolding was erected, building materials ordered and we set to work just the two of us without even a cement mixer to begin with as we had to budget quite carefully. Ruth used to be a nurse, she's given it up now, but at the time she would work just one night a week while I had a resident gig three evenings a week in a restaurant. I told you it was great being a musician! We had all week free to get on with the renovation work, although I wouldn't call it work; more like a way of life then.

Ruth proved to be the perfect grafter, helping to lump and heave all the building materials around. The old bath was still a usable item, but with no roof on the cottage, we would take our bath under the skies, after heating up the water on a camping stove. There is an RAF base nearby; I swear they would do their flying practice overhead just to catch glimpses of Ruth in the bath from above; she waved at one of the planes once, though I don't know how they knew when it was bath day!

#

In 1988 there was a slump in the housing market, which meant that we were unable to obtain a viable price for our recently rebuilt and modernised cottage, consequently, we decided to sit tight for a while, hoping that prices would pick up again. That of course left me at a bit of a loose end with regard to enterprise. I had started teaching again, but that was an evening activity. Part of the renovation work had included the barn, which I had made into a large workshop and then a nice little earner showed up in the form of buying and selling old pianos after giving them a bit of TLC. That worked out fine, it seemed like every church hall, and school wanted to practically give away their old Joana until one day I unknowingly sold a lady a piano which was badly riddled with woodworm inside. After an embarrassing confrontation with an irate husband who was backed up by a hysterical wife, I gave them their money back and decided not to get my hands burnt with anymore old pianos, subsequently giving that enterprise up.

The next venture was a winner; after finding that XK Jaguar 120 I told you about earlier. It had practically disintegrated into rust in some farm sheds, I put my old apprentice metal working skills to use and rebuilt it successfully; then had collectors lining up to buy it off me. I made contact with a trader in the USA who was selling left hand drive versions of many classic English sports cars. The internet hadn't arrived yet, but we did have fax machines on which I would receive pictures of the vehicles he was selling, then they would be shipped back across the Atlantic to the UK in a container, to be collected at the dock, piggy backed to North Yorkshire, and eventually, sold on to collectors after having had their bodies rebuilt in my workshop. Interested buyers would come from as far afield as Ireland and Hungary to acquire them. The only disaster to befall me during that little venture was an Austin-Healey breaking free from a pulley winch rope and careering down a hill that was our drive, crashing through a hedge then ending up in the field beyond with surprisingly little damage to the car. However, the bottom dropped out of the classic car market for a while in the nineties. Nothing good lasts forever does it? Hey, you can't win them all.

Chapter 33

Danni was born in '91, Ruth and I were quietly married the year before in a registry office. We had to ask one of the office girls to act as a witness because we didn't have a witness of our own. It was a beautiful early summer's day in June, making our cottage garden, where we took selfies with the timer on a 35mm camera afterwards, shine in the sunlight. We hadn't included Ruth's family in the occasion because of the antipathy felt by them towards me. When Ruth eventually broke the news to her parents, they made an effort to accept me and laid on a magnificent family and friend's party at their house in Leeds, it was really nice to be the guests of honour especially as previously they wouldn't give me the time of day.

Not long before she passed away, Ruth's mother took me to one side and confided to me how she thought we had two delightful daughters.

Stephanie arrived in '99, the last baby to be born in our village before the new millennium. The midwife wrapped her in a towel and placed her straight into my arms, as soon as she had popped out, because Ruth needed some medical attention. I was in awe of the whole experience even more when I felt the breath of our newly born baby on the side of my face, it inspired me to write a song 'Angel Breath On Me' the words and tune of which just came to me in a few minutes, seemingly with hardly any effort. Now that is what I call inspiration.

Ruth had not long given birth to Steph when we were on the move again… to the house next door. I recently was allowed a peek at the diary she was keeping when both Danni and Steph were born. She wrote how proud she was of me (she calls me Roddy) and how she couldn't have managed without me. I don't believe that for a minute about not managing without me, I think you girls have an inner strength that we fellas might find missing, but it did give me a certain pride in myself.

Oh! Yes, the house next door; not so much a house, more like a wooden chalet. It was originally owned by the same family who sold us the cottage we were leaving. We didn't need a removal van, as with the help of an eight-year-old Danielle, we carried all of our furniture and belongings from one house to the other across the two gardens, squashing some winter broccoli and sprout plants on the way.

I had set myself a pretty big building project to turn a wooden chalet into a proper brick and cobble house complete with a music studio and it took about eighteen months before the building dust had settled. However, it seems that no matter how hard I try, there always seems to be that nagging thought at the end of a project that this or that job could have been done a little different. I wonder what it takes to reach perfection in life….

Epilogue

I'm not going to tell you that life is easy, we all have our own cross to bear and each will tell you a different story. What I will tell you, is that believing in yourself and having a dream is real. Don't listen to anyone who says its pie in the sky, because that's nonsense. Life is for doing, otherwise what's the point? So do my friend, go on out and shake the tree.

> 'I have a balcony which looks down a road
> with flowers growing side by side.
> Along the road there is dust and confusion
> hiding the view that I have never seen,
> but I know the flowers still grow further down the road
> even though my eyes cannot see there.'
> Rod Graham

Please use this link to download the title track of the album:
Walk A Narrow Line.
http://www.walkanarrowline.com

Please use this link to access the whole album:
Walk A Narrow Line.
http://www.rod-graham.com